The Art and Science of Chess
A Step-by-Step Approach

The Art and Science of Chess

A Step-by-Step Approach

Robert Robinson   Raymond Edwards

HARPER & ROW, PUBLISHERS, INC.
New York, Evanston, San Francisco, London

Contents

PREFACE

This book is meant for the reader who knows nothing about chess, or who, having an elementary knowledge of the moves wishes to learn something of the principles behind the game. It is hoped that this book will also contain much of interest to the more experienced player, but it is written primarily for the beginner.

The great majority of novices are impatient and demand 'instant' chess. Of course they learn the moves of the chessmen and how to make captures. Though the idea of checkmate may be grasped, few beginners understand how to achieve it. Having jumped in at the deep end the young players fight for their lives in a kind of inverted losing game. There is horrific carnage on the chess board, strategy and tactics are restricted to attacks on the opponent's pieces, probably in the hope that such threats will not be noticed. It is all great fun and we agree that something may be learned in this way—but we do deprecate these practices, as they lead to bad habits and slow progress. Therefore, it is better to learn to walk before you learn to run. After all no one is placed at the head of a large army knowing nothing of the capabilities of the infantry, tanks and guns etc. under his command. But this is precisely the predicament in which a novice chess player often finds himself.

This book is planned as a progressive approach to chess, which proceeds step by step. We have tried to introduce chess ideas as early as possible, so as to arouse and maintain the interest of the reader. Accordingly, a short study of the powers of the pieces is presented and the first item, King and Rook v. King, was carefully selected as the best way of expounding the fundamentals of the game (Chapter 1). This is a novel approach and we attach great importance to the fact that chess play can be introduced after the first few pages and that exercises, which the student can work out for himself, can be suggested at this early stage.

The authors cannot overemphasise the importance of this

approach. The reader progressively learns the powers and possibilities of the pieces at his command so that, when he comes to command the complete chess army he will be able to conduct himself with credit. This method is in no way dull and unrewarding. For one thing there is much interesting chess play even in simplified positions and for another the student will avoid acquiring bad chess habits picked up in early random play. Happy the golfer who learnt the rudiments of a correct swing when he took up that game. Similarly with chess.

Following on from Chapter 1 the authors consider some tactical manoeuvres in Chapter 2. When he has mastered these the reader will be well able to appreciate the next three Sections which are devoted to the middle, opening and end game respectively. Reference can be made at this stage to the Games (Chapter 6) where subjects discussed in the text of Chapters 3, 4 and 5 are further considered during the course of actual master games.

By the end of Chapter 5 the reader who has followed the book in the proper sequence and has worked through the exercises, will be quite a competent player ready to play his first games. He might win, for not only will he be a much better player than the average beginner, but he will be able to hold his own with many club players.

The final section, Chapter 6, is a selection of master games, fully annotated, from Anderssen to Fischer. The games have been carefully chosen to illustrate the points made in earlier sections and are in fact cross-referenced to the appropriate parts of the text. In addition the games can be regarded as a short history of chess, showing briefly the evolution of the game in the last 150 years. The authors believe that the historical approach, which is one of the best teaching methods for any subject, is particularly applicable to chess. Indeed the view has been advanced that a chess player's natural development mirrors the history of the game. But apart from the didactic value, the games also flash and sparkle with the beauty and excitement of master chess. We are sure that the reader will also enjoy them.

The book concludes with a number of practical tips and a bibliography.

Acknowledgments

The authors wish to acknowledge the constructive advice of R. G. Wade who read the original manuscript and made many helpful suggestions which were incorporated in the final text; the co-operation of Peter Kemmis Betty of Batsford and the assistance of E. P. Muldoon in reading the proofs.

NOTES ON NOTATION

The chess world uses two systems of notation for recording chess moves. The most widely used is the algebraic. The so-called descriptive system is used only in English-speaking countries and Spain.

There is no doubt that the algebraic is the simplest and best system. It can be learnt by anyone (including non chess players) in about 60 seconds. Unquestionably beginners find it the easiest to learn.

The descriptive notation is more complicated, less precise and demands some knowledge of chess before it can be understood properly. The authors believe that the difficulty of the descriptive system has discouraged many beginners from taking up chess.

Therefore, the first two sections use the algebraic notation. However, as this book is written for English-speaking readers, the remaining sections employ the descriptive notation. The reader must be familiar with the descriptive as the overwhelming majority of chess books published for this market to date use that system. But by this stage the descriptive notation will be easily mastered by the reader. To resolve any ambiguities a game is given on Page 47 with the two notations side by side.

The use of algebraic notation is growing rapidly. The authors have little doubt that the descriptive notation will eventually become obsolete.

Symbols

+	Check
!	Strong move
!!	Very strong or brilliant move
?	Weak move
??	Blunder
!?	Double-edged or enterprising move
?!	Dubious move
1–0	Black resigned
$\frac{1}{2}$–$\frac{1}{2}$	Draw agreed
0–1	White resigned

W or B by the side of a diagram indicates which side is to move.

Numbers in brackets refer to the figure number of the relevant diagram.

1 The powers of the Pieces and Pawns; Illustrative Endings

A: PRELIMINARIES: KING AND ROOK

The Chess Board

Chess is played on a board divided into 64 squares. The squares of the board are conventionally described as white and black but they may be coloured in other ways (e.g. white and red, light and dark brown etc.). The board is placed at the commencement of a game so that a white square is in the corner on a player's right-hand side (diagram 1).

Black

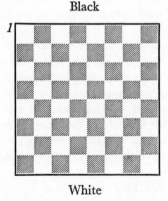

White

By convention in diagrams the white chessmen start from the bottom and the black men (a contraction of chessmen) from the top. Naturally the white player is supposed to look up the page in printed diagrams and the player of the black pieces is imagined to face him looking down.

Algebraic Notation, Part 1: The Board

In order to describe the position of the chessman and events on the board it is necessary to have a system of notation which will enable us to quickly identify the various squares. The algebraic system of notation has been internationally adopted for this purpose.

The terms *rank* and *file* are self-explanatory and these are numbered 1–8 and lettered a–h respectively, as shown in diagram 2.

For example the crossed squares, left to right, are a2, b6, c4, d3, e8, f1, g5, h7. It is helpful to visualise the ranks and files as groups of 4 thus: 1, 2, 3, 4 and 5, 6, 7, 8; a, b, c, d and e, f, g, h, so that it will be unnecessary to

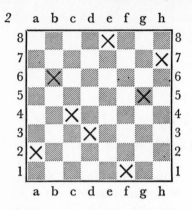

work this out laboriously each time you need to locate one of these ranks or files.

All the squares are uniquely described in this way as the intersection of a numbered rank and a lettered file. This logical device is easy to use and is standard in most countries. It has about the same relation to the more cumbrous British and American nomenclature (see p. 45) as the metric system has to that of our weights and measures. We shall use the algebraic notation in this chapter and in Chapter 2, chiefly because it is easiest for the reader to understand.

The Chess Pieces

Before examining the moves and powers of the various pieces in detail, it is well to discuss some of the features they have in common.

Each chessman in play occupies one of the squares of the board and no two men may stand on the same square. If, for example, a white piece or pawn already stands on any square, say d4, then another white piece would be unable to play to d4. Without exception the players move alternately; there is no privilege allowing a player two or more moves in succession.

If in the exercise of its lawful powers a piece could move into a certain square, it is said to *command* that square, and to *attack* a hostile unit or to *protect* a friendly unit on that square.

Capturing. Captures are made by moving a man into a square occupied by a hostile unit. The captured man is removed from the board, and the capturing piece takes its place. Captures are indicated by the sign x which means 'takes' placed between the symbol for the piece taking and the reference to the square on which the captured piece is placed.

At this stage we will concentrate on only two pieces, namely the king, the most important of them all, and another, the rook. With the help of these two pieces it will be possible to explain most of the underlying principles of the game.

The King (symbolised by K). The move of the king is simple, namely one square in any direction. In the centre of the board the unimpeded king has 8 moves, at the edge of the board he has 5 possible moves and in the corner only 3.

The Rook* (symbolised by R). The rook moves along a rank or file, any number of squares from one to seven, so long as the path is unimpeded. It is not able to jump over any man in its way and the rook effects a capture by displacing a hostile man as the result of a legal move parallel to one of the sides of the board. Each player has two rooks at the commencement of a game, placed on a1 and h1 for the white player and a8 and h8 for black.

Diagram 3 illustrates the moves of king and rook.

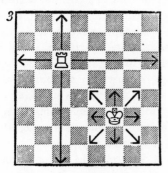

Check and Checkmate

(Check is symbolised by +)
The king is the most important of all the pieces because the object of the game is to capture the king and the game is won when one

* A rook was formerly called 'castle', a form still preferred by children.

side captures the king of the opposing forces. But actually a *punctilio* of great delicacy is observed. The game is won when the capture of the hostile king is seen to be unavoidable. When, in the sense already explained, a hostile chessman commands the square on which a king stands, that king is said to be in *check*. The player making the move which attacks the king should call 'check'. The king or his men must at once take some measures to remove the check. This could only be by one of the following means:
(a) Moving the king to a square not commanded by a hostile chessman.
(b) By capturing the piece that checked (attacked) the king.
(c) By interposing a chessman between the attacking man and the square attacked and on which the king stands. As explained on p. 13 a check from the chessman called knight cannot be met by interposition.

If none of these measures is possible, then the situation is called *checkmate* and the game is over, the player of the checkmated king has lost.

It is very important to note firstly that the check must be neutralised immediately: a king is not allowed to remain in check for a single move; secondly, at no stage may the king move into check, nor may any of his allied forces move so as to disclose check on his majesty.

Furthermore, there is no tit for tat in this matter of checkmate. If your king is checkmated in a certain number of moves it is irrelevant that you could reply by a checkmate having taken the same number of moves. The game was finished when you were checkmated.

It is an obvious consequence of these rules that the kings can never come into contact, that is, occupy adjoining squares. Again, a king cannot capture a hostile man which is protected by another man. That would be a forbidden play into check.

Algebraic Notation, Part 2: The Pieces

We have shown earlier (p. 1–2) how the squares on the board may be identified. Now we explain how the moves of the pieces are described.

In the algebraic system a move is indicated by writing first the symbol for the piece (e.g. in the case of the King—K). Following the piece symbol there is the square to which the piece is played. For example, Kd2 means that the king moves to d2. During the course of a game (or from a diagram) we always know whence the piece has come. But when there are two or more men of the same kind on the board, it may be that more than one such piece could play to the designated square. This ambiguity is avoided by writing the file of origin after the piece symbol then the square of arrival on completion of the move. For example, Rad2. Anticipating a little of what quickly follows, there might be another rook on e2, f2, g2 or h2 or on a square of the d-file which could also move to d2. This method is adopted in cases of ambiguity only.

Checkmate of Black King by White King and Rook

We are now in a position to study some real chess play and to learn how checkmate can be forced by the stronger party in what is called the endgame or ending. For clarity of exposition we assume that the white king is attempting to mate his black counterpart but, of course, the reverse could apply.

It is decidedly advantageous for the beginner to learn how to play with just a few pieces before attempting to cope with the problems involved in handling the full complement of men at his command at the beginning of the game.

The present example is not at all a rare outcome of a game and it is important to grasp the principles of the methods used and then to practise them until mate (short for checkmate) can be effected with ease and certainty. In this way a definite step forward will have been taken, since it will be necessary to 'see ahead' and to make calculations, even though these may be relatively simple ones.

First, consider the problem when the black king is in the middle of the board, say at d5. It is the rook which must give check and hence the rook can only cover two of the king's eight flight squares (or four if the rook is adjacent to the king). The rook does cover two of the squares because, although the rook cannot jump to the square beyond the king, it is covered for the present purpose. Suppose the last move of the rook has brought it to g5. Then this move brought the rook to a square where he has a legal move to d5. In a word the king is in check. Evidently he cannot avoid this threat by moving to e5 which is still in the line of the rook's fire. But he cannot go to c5 either because, after d5 is vacated, c5 is also commanded by the rook. So long as the rook gives check to the king he cannot improve on this performance, that is coverage of only two flight squares.

The king may be brought in to help, but the best he can do is to cover three flight squares of the

king. In diagram 4 these squares (king at d3) are c4, d4, and e4. The flight squares still available are c6, d6 and e6.

The only possible resource is to drive the black king to one of the four sides of the board when only five flight squares are available, the other three having, as it were, been pushed over the edge where the black king cannot follow them.

Diagram 5 imagines that such a position has been achieved and shows the black king checkmated by the white king and rook.

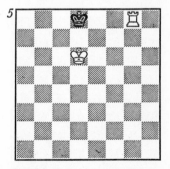

In the first place the king is in check from the rook and secondly he is unable to move to any square which is not covered either by the white king or by the rook.

The impossibility of moving along the line of fire of the rook must always be remembered. We shall see later that the same consideration applies to other long range pieces. We will now examine the methods used to bring about this checkmate. They are so well understood that a player, reduced to lone king against his opponent's king and rook, normally resigns.

Let us suppose that the black king is on the eighth rank, say at c8; he can be held to this rank by a rook on the seventh rank, say at a7. Evidently the king cannot move into the seventh rank with the object of crossing it because that would be moving into check, which is prohibited. To complete the picture we place the white king at e5. It is quite an arbitrary choice. (diagram 6).

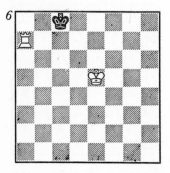

Play might proceed as follows:

1 Kd6 Kb8 2 Rh7 (N.B. the black king threatened to capture the rook which, therefore, moves out of danger, preserving control of the black king moves—that is keeping the king confined to the eighth rank. If white were foolish enough to play, say, 2 Kc6? Black would play 2 ... K×a7 capturing the rook) 2 ... Kc8 3 Rg7 (this is a waiting move motivated by White noticing that 3 ... Kd8? 4 Rg8 gives checkmate—as in diagram 5, please verify! Hence the black king must move to b8, the only alternative.) 3 ... Kb8 4 Kc6 Ka8 (again if 4 ... Kc8 5 Rg8 mate) 5 Kb6 Kb8 6 Rg8 mate.

The idea underlying the 'waiter' 3 Rg7 is now clear. It was a matter of correct timing and the scheme adopted was to force the mating position by the rebound after the king reached the corner. This bounce back is often the quickest method once the king is confined to one of the sides of the board.

Another extremely useful 'waiter' is illustrated if we place the white king at f3, the white rook at e1 and the black king at h2. In order to mate the king we need to force him to h3, which happens at the moment to be the only square to which he can move as the rook controls g1 and h1. All we need to do is to hold the position. But White must move.

The solution is to move the rook to the left, e.g. to a1. Now 1 Ra1 Kh3 2 Rh1 mate.

The positions arising in actual play will rarely be the most favourable. Thus, if the black king is on e5, the white king and rook on b2 and a1 respectively, the position is about as good for Black as possible. Yet he loses quickly. Play might proceed: 1 Kc3 (the rook can do nothing without the king, hence the white king must be brought into active play as quickly as possible). 1 . . . Ke4 2 Ra5 (now the rook restricts the freedom of the black king) 2 . . . Ke3 3 Re5+ Kf4 4 Kd4 Kf3 5 Re8 (waiter) 5 . . . Kf2 6 Kd3 Kf3 7 Rf8+ Kg4 8 Ke4 Kg3 9 Rf4 Kg2 10 Ke3 Kg1 11 Rf2 Kh1 12 Kf3 Kg1 13 Kg3 Kh1 14 Rf1 mate.

Or black might play 1 . . . Kd5 2 Ra5+ Ke6 3 Kd4 Kf6 4 Ke4 Kg6 5 Kf4 Kf6 6 Ra6+ Kf7 7 Ke5 Kg7 8 Kf5 Kf7 9 Ra7+ and with the king now driven to the back rank mate is forced as previously. The method is always to combine the king and rook in such a way that they progressively hem in and confine the opposing monarch until he is forced to one of the sides of the board. Once this has been achieved mate follows quickly.

This part of our exposition must be studied and practised until full mastery has been obtained; a great deal of chess will be learned in the process.

Drawn Games

If in the examples of mate given above the white player allowed his rook to be captured, then both players would be left with only their kings. In such a position neither side can force mate and the game is drawn. Any reduction in the forces to such a level that mate cannot be effected, leaves a drawn game. A clearance leaving only king v. king is obviously a case in point. Other ways in which a game may be drawn are discussed on p. 28.

Stalemate

If a player whose turn it is to move, and whose king is not in check, has no legal move, the game is drawn. This situation is called *stalemate*, a word that has passed into the language for more general use. Imagine a white king at c6, rook at b7 and black king at a8. If it were Black's turn to move he could not do so, as any move would be a move into check. He is therefore in stalemate and the game is drawn. However, if it is White to move, any rook move would release the stalemate and White could mate quickly; but if White played Kb6? he would not release the stalemate and the game would be drawn.

Exercises

Important Note: The exercises and solutions should be read and studied as part of the text. They are not so much riddles as further developments and are separated from the text so as to give the reader the opportunity to attempt the solutions for himself. Solutions to all exercises are given on p. 130.

Exercise 1

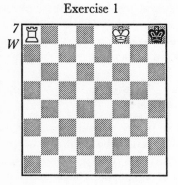

White to play and mate in three moves. This means (1) White plays and then Black plays; (2) White plays, Black plays; (3) White plays, giving checkmate. How many solutions are there? Give White's first move only.

Ex. 2: White king to play and mate in ten moves or less

Ex. 3: In how many moves can White effect checkmate, given best play by Black?

Exercise 2

Exercise 3

The Opposition

A king cannot lay itself open to capture and hence cannot touch the hostile king (c.f. p. 4). So when the two kings, both on the same rank or file, get as close together as possible, that is are separated by one square, the king having the move must give way by retreat or by moving aside. For example, white king f4, black king f6. If it is Black's turn to move, he must play to either e6 or g6 or the 7th rank when White can advance; thus 1 ... Kg6 2 Ke5. The king *not* having the move, with one square separation is said to have the *opposition*. A player who is able to move his king so that he stands one square removed from the other king, both on the same rank or file, is said to be able to *seize the opposition*.

If an uneven number of squares greater than 1 stands between the kings, the player not having the move has the *distant opposition*. This has the property that it can be converted into close opposition if the hostile king attempts an approach. This then could be a separation of 5 squares and we assume it is the turn of the black king to move, e.g. white king f2, black king f8, White has the distant opposition. Then suppose Black approaches to 4 square separation 1 ... Kf7 White replies by moving forward to 3 square separation 2 Kf3. It is still Black's turn to move and White still has the distant opposition. A second approach by Black 2 ... Kf6 will enable White to reply 3 Kf4, seizing the close opposition.

Ex. 4: White to play and win using the rook once only to administer the final checkmate. This exercise is a study in the distant opposition and White's first move must therefore be 1 Kh2, seizing the distant opposition.

(a) How does White then win and in how many moves can mate be reached?

Exercise 4

(b) If White plays 1 Kg1, how would Black draw (under the condition laid down re passivity of rook)?
(c) If White played 1 Kg2, how would Black draw under the conditions?

The Two Rooks

We have mentioned above that each player has two rooks at the commencement of the game. The next three exercises illustrate the great power the two rooks can exert when they work together.

Exercise 5

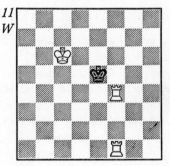

White to play and mate in two moves

Exercise 6

White to play and mate in two moves

Exercise 7

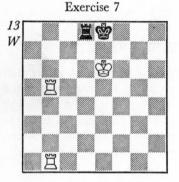

White mates in four moves (two solutions). Of course it is easy to win with a rook in hand, but to mate in four it is necessary to play a rook to the g-file; either 1 Rg1 or 1 Rg4. Assuming 1 Rg1 work out the subsequent play, giving mate in three more moves.

Exercise 8

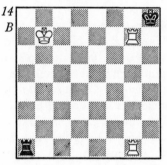

Black to play and draw. The black king has no move but it is not stalemate because Black has a rook on a1. So what? The solution may involve captures.

B: BISHOPS, QUEENS AND KNIGHTS

The reader will remember that in section A we considered the moves of two of the chess pieces, the king and rook. In fact at the beginning of the game a player has five more, namely two bishops, a queen and two knights. This section deals with the powers and characteristics of these pieces.

The Bishop (symbolised by B)

The bishop moves and captures diagonally. Its moves are illustrated in diagram 15.

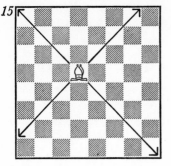

black king occupies a corner square.

The white bishops start on c1 and f1 and the black bishops on c8 and f8. Bishops, therefore, unlike rooks, are always limited to the squares having the colour of that on which they start the game. It will be seen that c1 is a conventional black square and f1 is a white square. On the black side the colours are reversed.

King and bishop cannot mate a king when the three pieces stand alone on the board. This is not a question of good or bad play, it cannot be done even accidentally. Hence king and bishop v. king is drawn by reason of insufficient force to effect mate.

King and two bishops v. king can force a mate but it is not particularly easy nor is it frequently encountered as an endgame. It is possible to set up a mate with king at the side of the board but, as a general rule, this cannot be obtained in play. A mating position that can be forced by a sequence of legal moves is that shown in diagram 16 in which the

The exact position of the bishops is immaterial but they must be in command of the diagonals indicated. The final moves by which diagram 16 was reached can be deduced by retrogressive analysis. The last move must have been Be4 mate and before that the black king moved from b8 to a8. But this is in the line of fire of the bishop at f4, which accordingly must have moved to this square to give check. Unless the white-squared bishop were then at f5 the king would have had a choice.

Thus we get back to diagram 17.

The final moves are: 1 Bf4+ Ka8 2 Be4 mate.

These bishop checks on adjacent diagonals are analogous to the rook checks on adjacent ranks or files but are much harder to manage. Keeping the idea of the mate in mind it should be possible

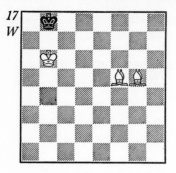

to drive the king to a corner and checkmate him.

One example of the process must suffice as the practical significance of the operation is more as a hint of a type of combination in the middle game than for the actual end games. (diagram 18).

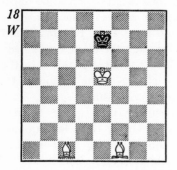

White to play and mate in eleven moves. White mates as follows: 1 Bh3 Kf7 2 Bf5 Ke7 3 Bg5+ Ke8 (or 3 ... Kf7 4 Bf6) 4 Ke6 Kf8 5 Bg6 Kg7 6 Bh5 Kf8 7 Kf6 Kg8 8 Bh6 Kh7 9 Kg5 Kg8 10 Kg6 (now that the black king is penned in the corner, White rearranges his pieces in order to

give mate) 10 ... Kh8 11 Bd1 Kg8 12 Bb3+ Kh8 13 Bg7 mate.

The Queen (symbolised by Q)

The queens are the most powerful of the pieces, combining the moves of rook and bishop. They can move any number of squares in any direction. The white queen starts the game on d1 and the black queen on d8. Owing to her great range of action the queen is used more often than any other piece to give the final blow of checkmate.

The moves of the queen are illustrated in diagram 19.

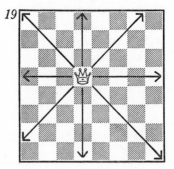

It should be noted, however, that even the king and queen cannot checkmate the opposing king in mid-board; it is necessary to drive the king to a side square. When effecting mate the queen, which has the powers of a rook, can be used in much the same way. The danger of stalemate is, however, greater and must be carefully avoided.

For example, if the white king is at e5, the queen at d6 and the black king at e8, White must not play his king to e6 or f6 because the result is a draw by stalemate. The better course would be 1 Qc7 Kf8 2 Kf6. If the reply is 2 ... Ke8 White mates either by 3 Qc8, using the diagonal command of d7 by the queen as well as the rook-like functions along the eighth rank, or by 3 Qe7, a characteristic close contact mate by a protected queen. If 2 ... Kg8 3 Qg7 mate, again by the 'kiss of death'. This type of mate by the queen is extremely common and naturally the support need not be given by the king—any piece will serve the purpose of protection to prevent ... K×Q.

The Knight (symbolised by N)

At the beginning the knights stand, between the bishops and rooks, on b1 and g1 (b8 and g8 for the black knights). The move is to the opposite corner of a rectangle of five squares (diagram 20).

The move may be made in any direction and the knight can jump over pieces on intervening squares. The knight is the only piece that has this peculiar power.

Captures, checks and protection follow the usual rule. Thus captures can be made on the square to which the knight can be

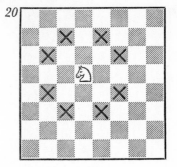

played. If a black king were on f6 in diagram 20, it would be in check from the white knight at d5. Interposition between knight and king does not parry a check. The only courses open are to move the king to a square not commanded by a piece or to capture the knight.

Even two knights and king cannot by themselves force checkmate and a reduction to these forces is therefore a draw. The knight, however, co-operates very well with other pieces, especially the queen, and is of great importance in tactical manoeuvres.

King, bishop and knight can mate the lone king but it is a very difficult task. The king must first be driven into a corner commanded by the bishop. The white king is a knight move from the corner and the bishop is so placed as to allow the opposing king to oscillate. In diagram 21 these squares are g8 and h8, the knight may be on any square, say d3.

21

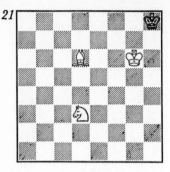

space which would be needed for a comprehensive discussion.

Exercise 9

22
W

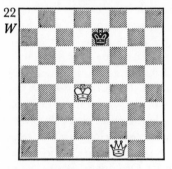

White to play and mate in at most four moves

Exercise 10

23
W

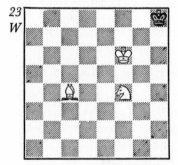

It is desired to play Nh6+ when Black's king is at g8. It will be found by trial that the knight can only reach h6 from d3 in an *odd* number of moves, however tortuous the route. For example N–f2–g4–h6—three moves or N–b2–a4–c3–e2–g3–f5–h6—seven moves. Thence if 1 Nf2 Kg8 2 Ng4 Kh8 3 Nh6 stalemate. The timing is wrong in this case, as the knight cannot lose a move. This property of the knight is sometimes called 'invariability of the knight move'.

It is necessary to lose a move with the bishop at some stage, for example: 1 Nf2 Kg8 2 Ng4 Kh8 3 Bb4 (the waiter) 3 . . . Kg8 4 Nh6+ Kh8 5 Bc3 mate.

Closing the mating net with king, bishop and knight v king involves some tricky manoeuvres, when the king is forced to the side of the board it should make for the wrong corner, that which is not of the same colour as the hostile bishop. As a general problem this ending hardly justifies the

Exercise 11

24
W

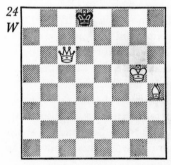

Ex. 10: White to play and mate. This is quite difficult; the student should study the solution in order to understand how the three white pieces co-operate to force mate on the black king. (*22*)

Ex. 11: Mate in how many moves? (**24**)

C: THE PAWNS

At the commencement of a game a player has at his command, in addition to the pieces described in the two previous sections, eight pawns (symbolised by P). At the commencement of a game the eight white pawns occupy the 2nd rank and correspondingly the eight black pawns are on the 7th rank. They are designated according to the file on which they stand.

A white pawn moves only up the file and can never come back. The short rook-like moves may be of one or two squares on the *first move* of a pawn at any stage of the game. Subsequent moves are of one square only at a time. The black pawns move in exactly the same manner but come down the file.

Pawns never make a diagonal move except to capture and they can *only* capture by one diagonal move, either side, in the general direction of their progress.

Diagram 25 illustrates the various moves of the pawn. The white pawn d2 moves to d4; a move to d3 was also possible. This shorter move is shown by the black pawn d7–d6. The black king on f6 is not in check from the pawn at f5

even though the latter could move to f6, if and when the king vacates the square. At the moment the pawn f5 is blocked by the king and cannot move to f6. Next, the white pawn on a4 can capture the black rook at b5, similarly the black pawn at f3 can capture the bishop at g2. Finally, the white king at h4 is in check from the black pawn at g5.

25
W

Under the algebraic system the *P* symbol is not normally used. The move 1 Pd2–d4 is shortened to 1 d4. In the case of captures the original square from which the pawn moves may be given: c3×d4, or one of two conventional abbreviations may be used: c×d4, or simply cd.

Capture made 'en passant'

If a white pawn stands on the fifth rank, a black pawn on an adjacent file could make a first move from the seventh rank to the fifth. In doing so the black pawn would pass the white pawn, and so deprive it of the possible capture which could follow a pawn move to the sixth rank. Under such circumstances the white pawn may capture the black pawn as it passes. The black pawn is removed from the board and the white pawn makes a one-square diagonal move forwards.

In diagram 25 Black's last move could have been g7–g5+. The white pawn at f5 can reply f5×g6*ep*, occupying g6. Advantage of the *en passant* rule must be taken at once. If the special capture is not made on the move following that of the enemy pawn, it cannot be made at all.

For a black pawn the situation is reversed; the black pawn standing on the fourth rank captures *en passant* a white pawn that moves from the second to the fourth rank on an adjacent file. For example, white pawn d2, black pawn e4: 1 d4 e4×d3*ep*.

Promotion of a Pawn

When a white pawn reaches the eighth rank it can, and must, be exchanged for a queen, rook, bishop or knight. A black pawn is similarly promoted on reaching the first rank. The promotion ranks may be reached by normal pawn moves or by captures. Pieces gained by promotion may be additional to the original complement of pieces.

In nearly every case a player will prefer to take a queen for his promoted pawn, but there are exceptional positions in which it is better to take either a rook, or a bishop or a knight. For example, a P to rank 8=Q could stalemate the king. P=R might avoid this and still be enough to win the game. Perhaps the most common alternative is P=N in a position where the knight would give check and the queen would not. P=Q is, however, the normal promotion and the operation is called 'queening the pawn'.

King and Pawn Ending

It is true that many games end by some spectacular checkmate with many pieces on the board; a finish in the middle of the battle as it were. Nevertheless the great majority of properly conducted and defended games are struggles for material advantage and the 'queening of a pawn' becomes an objective in very many cases. This tilts the scales decisively in favour of the side gaining a new queen. The new queen mops up the remaining opposing pieces and pawns and quickly makes it possible to impose checkmate. It is therefore of vital importance to know how to manage pawns with a view to promotion and there are certain standard positions which must be studied, and memorised so that they become part of one's second nature—from a chess point of view.

The first thing to note is that the kings are frequently the only pieces left that can be used to catch and capture a pawn if it races for the promotion rank. Let us see how successful, or otherwise, a king is in pursuit of a pawn.

Inspection and trial will show that it is always possible for the king to capture the pawn if he can play into the square (or squares) of which a side is formed by the pawn and its promotion position (diagram 26).

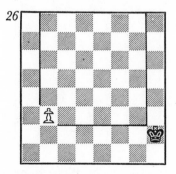

26

Here the pawn at b3 queens at b8. The king at h2 with move must play to g3 and then when

the pawn advances will play along the diagonal of the square and will be able to capture the promoted pawn at b8. If the king had been able to play to e3 the capture would occur on b6. On the other hand, if the pawn has the move in diagram 26, it can queen and cannot be caught by the king at h2, or indeed if the king is anywhere on the first or second ranks or on the h-file.

This is just king v. pawn and, although the aforementioned 'square of squares' is an essential element in our calculations, there are many circumstances that may affect the issue. Thus the black king in diagram 26 could be blocked by one of his own pawns, say on d6 (not represented in the diagram). This pawn could race its opposite number to queen; but if we assume the white king to be placed at b1 that monarch can move to stop and capture this pawn on the d-file. Moreover, if the player of the black pieces moves d6–d5, in order to get out of the way of his king at h2, the king will be that one move too late and the white pawn will queen on b8 with impunity.

King and Pawn v. King

Every chess player must be familiar with this ending. Naturally the lone king makes for his base line and hopes to occupy the queening square. Only in one case does this inevitably draw the game. If the advancing pawn is on files a or h (R-files), the defending king always draws if he can reach the corner. The attempt to drive him out results in stalemate (cf. p. 7).

In discussing king and rook v. king an example of the importance of the opposition of kings was mentioned (see p. 8 above). This property of kings is a consequence of the fact that they may not come into contact. Hence, if separated by one square or a file (the more important case in the present analysis), the player with the move must retreat or move to an adjacent file. Naturally it is possible to lose and regain the opposition if a spare move with another man is available. This spare move is frequently provided by the pawn and may be used with advantage unless it has advanced too far. The following positions illustrate the more important cases.

In diagram 27 White, to play, wins by 1 b7 Ka7 (forced) 2 Kc7 Ka6 3 b8=Q, and in this particular position mate follows quickly by 3 . . . Ka5 4 Qb3 Ka6 5 Qb6 mate or 5 Qa4 mate.

The rule is that in advancing to the seventh rank from the sixth, protected by the king, the pawn *must not give check*. Thus in diagram 27, if it is Black to move, White cannot win. Play continues 1 . . . Kc8 2 b7+ Kb8 3 Kb6—otherwise the black king will be able to capture the pawn, but the position after 3 Kb6 is stalemate.

Now in diagram 27, keep the pawn on b6, but start with the white king on b5 and the black on b7. Black to move. The question is should he play to b8 or c8. Obviously it must be b8 because after Kc6 he can reply . . . Kc8, leading to the drawn position.

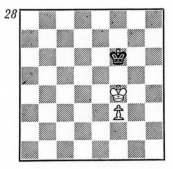

In diagram 28, White to move can only draw. Black has the opposition and can maintain it. E.g. 1 Kg4 Kg6 2 f4 (the only

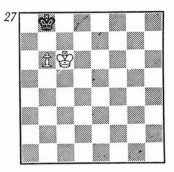

way to vary, the play of king always facing king in the 'opposition' manner) 2 ... Kf6 3 f5 Kf7 4 Kg5 Kg7 (regaining the 'opposition') 5 f6+ Kf7 6 Kf5 Kf8 7 Kg6 drawing as above. But if Black has the move, White has the 'opposition' and Black must retreat or give way to the side. White can then advance his king and pawn so as to queen the pawn. As this is such a vitally important matter we consider two variations.

In the first Black retreats and hopes in so doing to break away and capture the pawn with the king too far advanced. He is unable to realise such a scheme: 1 ... Kf7 2 Kf5 Kf8 3 Kf6 now Black *must* go sideways, e.g. 3 ... Kg8 4 f4 Kf8 5 f5 Kg8. We have repeated this king against king relation after move 3, but the pawn is two squares nearer home. So now 6 Ke7 and the pawn under protection of the king marches home to f8 and queens, wherever the black king is played. Moreover, there is no chance of stalemate.

In the second variation Black endeavours to oppose the white king more directly. 1 ... Kg6' 2 Ke5 Kg5 3 f4+ Kg6 4 Ke6 Kg7 5 f5 Kf8 6 Kf6 Kg8 (or mirror image 6 ... Ke8) 7 Ke7 and the pawn goes through to queen.

It is instructive to note that in diagram 28 if the white pawn stood on f2 instead of f3, then White wins with or without the move. The reasoning is as follows: If it is White to play 1 f3 produces diagram 28 and it is Black's move, which we have seen loses for him. If it is Black's turn to play, then White has the opposition and the option of f2–f4 instead of f3–f4 in the variations given above. This analysis is an illustration of the value of a spare pawn move in endings of this type.

There are so many 'buts' in chess and here is one. If the white king as well as pawn is too far back, the black king may be able to secure the opposition and draw the game. For example: White: King e2, pawn d2; Black: king d7. Black to play and draw. 1 ... Ke6 seizing the 'distant opposition'. White cannot turn the tables by using his spare pawn move in this case as his king is not placed very well. Thus 2 Ke3 Ke5 3 d3 Kd5 4 d4 Kd6 5 Ke4 Ke6 drawn as aforesaid (q.v.). However, if the black king stood originally on d8 or c8, White would win with 1 Kd3 or 1 Ke3 respectively. The improved position of the white king opposite his black counterpart enables him to win the game and not submit to a draw as previously.

Endings in which both sides are left with one or more pawns, but without pieces, are very often reached. Other factors need to be considered in endings of this type and for this reason further attention is paid to these positions in Chapter 2 (pp. 31–47).

Nevertheless, we may study two compositions which, with the simple material of king and pawn v. king and pawn, are both elegant and difficult to solve.

29
W

The first, by Reti, is shown in diagram 29. The problem is: White to play and Black to draw. The position looks hopeless for Black, since the white a–pawn can race up its file to queen and the black pawn appears to be neutralised by the white king which is in the 'pawn square' and can capture it, if advanced, on f1. Naturally White plays 1 a4. The key to Black's resource is that he can gain time to get his king into the 'pawn square' by threatening to support his own pawn and to queen it. Therefore 1 ... Kb2 2 a5 Kc3 3 a6 Kd2 4 a7 f2 5 Kg2 Ke1 and both pawns queen—drawn. One

alternative in this is 3 Kg3 Kd4 4 K×f3 Kc5 and wins the pawn— draw. The principle is always the same, namely defence by counter-attack. The reader may wish to work out other alternatives and find the drawing moves.

The second position (diagram 30) by Grigoriev, shows what may happen when both pawns queen but the king and queen of one party are particularly unfavourably disposed.

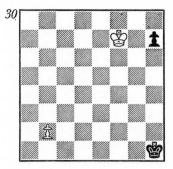

30

White achieves nothing by advancing his pawn to queen, as Black does likewise. Therefore 1 Kf6 Kg2 2 b4 h5 3 Kg5 Kg3. All this is quite natural play but now White must decide whether he should take the black pawn or not. If he does, a draw will result as the black king can move into the 'square' of the white pawn by Kf4 and will stop and capture the pawn. If White allows the black pawn to queen it will do so later than his own b8=Q and the draw will still be in hand. There is, however, a win available. The solution continues 4 b5 h4 5 b6 h3 6 b7 h2 7 b8=Q+ Kg2 8 Qb2+ Kg1 (What else? 8 ... Kh1 blocks the pawn and 8 ... Kh3 allows 9 Qb7 preventing the pawn from queening) 9 Kg4! h1=Q 10 Kg3! This fine move is the culmination of White's strategy. Mate follows in one or two moves and can only be briefly postponed by sacrifice of the black queen.

We are sure that readers will agree that these two studies are both artistic and instructive. There are many more that are equally meritorious, involving exact calculation and deep insight. In fact pawn play is an advanced aspect of chess, analogous perhaps to the use of the pedal on the pianoforte. There is nothing that distinguishes the master from the amateur more clearly than his quick grasp of the end game and especially pawn play.

Exercise 13

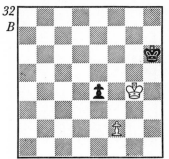

Black to play and draw

Exercise 14

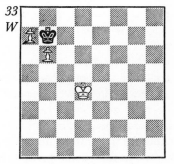

White to play and win

Exercise 12

White to play and win

Exercise 15

White to play and win

Exercise 16

35
W

White to play and draw. White's problem is how to defend himself against the threat of 1 ... Kh2 followed by the queening of the g–pawn (Study by Henri Rinck)

D: PAWNS WITH PIECES

This topic covers a large part of tactics and strategy in chess and is dealt with later in greater detail.

At this stage a few cases in which one or more pawns have resources against pieces are noted. The main purpose of this exposition is twofold. First it is to enable the student to gain further practice in the handling of pieces and pawns and by so doing gain an understanding of their various strengths and weaknesses. Second, an introduction is given to some of the resources that abound in the end game. A player who knows these resources will win or draw many games he would otherwise fail to win, or even lose.

Knights v. Pawns

Owing to its peculiar move a knight is sometimes unable to stop a pawn even though it may appear to be near enough to do so. For example, a pawn at a5 with move can queen at a8 despite the efforts of a knight at f3. 1 a6 Nd4 2 a7 Nc6 3 a8=Q. This assumes that the kings are mere spectators. Suppose, however, that the white king is at c2 and the black king at e8. Then 1 a6 Nd4+ 2 Kc3 Nc6 3 Kc4 Kd7 4 Kb5 Kc7. In this case Black gained a move by means of a check and the knight arrived in time to stop further advance. Of course, knight and king has no hope of winning v. king and if the pawn advanced ... N×P would have to be played (queen and king win against king and knight). The simple way to ensure the draw would be for Black to play Na7 and back to c6.

Another effect of the short-stepping nature of the knight's move is that the unaided knight often finds great difficulty in stopping a passed pawn supported by its king. While a queen, rook or bishop can stop a pawn at a distance, a knight must be close at hand. And if the knight's freedom to manoeuvre is restricted by the opposing king, then the knight may be unable to stop the pawn. An example is the rook pawn where the knight is further handicapped by the lack of space at the edge of the board. White: K at h8, N at a1; Black: K at a3, P at a2. Black to play wins by . . . Kb2 and even with the move White cannot save himself after 1 Nc2+ Kb2 and the knight must abandon command of the corner square or be captured.

Bishops v. Pawns

As will be readily realised, the bishop has no difficulty in stopping a passed pawn. It is simply played to a position from which it can command one of the squares over which the pawn will have to pass on its journey to queen. The mobility of the bishop enables it to do this from the far side of the board if necessary away from the opposing king, and it thus has none of the difficulties experienced by the knight.

However, the major weakness of the bishop—the fact that it can control only either the black or white squares—is particularly noticeable in some endings. Thus,

white king, bishop and pawn win easily against the lone king, provided the pawn is secure. There are two positions, however, where the superior party, despite his large preponderance in material, cannot win.

Firstly—a rook pawn, moving to queen where the queening square is not commanded by the bishop. The defending king makes for the queening square and once there the game is drawn because he can always move out of the corner and back again. If he *cannot* move from the corner he is stalemated.

Exercise 17

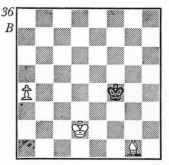

36
B

Is the result of the game affected if the white pawn stood at a3 rather than a4?

Secondly—there is a unique position in which a king, bishop and pawn on a knight file (b or g) cannot force a win. White: K any, bishop a7, pawn b6; Black: king a8. If the white king moves so as to command a7, stalemate results. The only attempt to make progress is to play Bb8, allowing K×b8, but the resulting position will always be drawn in accordance with the principles already discussed under *King and Pawn v. King* (p. 17).

A bishop has great difficulty in stopping two disconnected passed pawns if they are far advanced and widely separated: White: king at d1, pawns a6 and f5; Black: king d3, bishop d4. White wins by 1 f6 B×f6 2 a7 and the pawn queens. Note that 1 a7 B×a7 2 f6 Bc5 only draws, as the bishop commands the queening square. This kind of combination is quite common.

Rook v. Pawns

Stopping a passed pawn presents no problems to a rook. However, a pawn supported by a king and sufficiently far advanced and removed from the opposing king will usually draw against a rook, as the rook is unable to prevent the pawn from queening. The rook must capture the pawn even though recapture by the king is inevitable. This follows from the fact that king and queen win against king and rook.

It is easy to see that two (or more) unconnected pawns would be helpless against a rook that could command the queening

Black to play and draw

rank (or any other that the pawns have not yet reached). The rook could sweep up the pawns as they were advanced, one after another (the contrast with the bishop's powers is most instructive). But once the pawns are connected the rook has much more trouble. In fact, two connected passed black pawns on the third rank win against an unaided rook. Similarly, two adjacent white pawns on the sixth rank win against the rook. In both cases the pawns must be out of the rook's range, i.e. it must not be possible to play 1 R×P. The connected pawns can support each other and the rook can never be so deployed as to enable it to capture both pawns. Diagram 38 illustrates a typical position.

White to play cannot prevent one of the pawns from queening. For example:

(a) 1 Rb3 e2 2 R×f3 e1=Q or;

(b) 1 Rb1 e2 2 Re1 f2 3 R×e2
f1 = Q, and finally;
(c) 1 Rb7+ Kg6 2 Re7 f2 3 R×e3
f1 = Q.

Queen v. Pawns

Since the queen is much the most
powerful of the pieces, it is
naturally the most successful in
stopping a passed pawn. In fact
the queen is the only piece able to
stop a passed pawn on the seventh
rank even when that pawn is
supported by its king. The procedure the queen employs is a
series of checks and threats to
capture the pawn which eventually forces the opposing king to
occupy the queening square. This
naturally removes the power of
the pawn to queen. The other
king can then move in to the kill.
Repetition of this process enables
the king to contact the pawn from
any distance. The queen can then
take the pawn, being protected by
its own king.

While the method outlined
above is always successful with
pawns on files b, d, e or g, it does
not apply to those on the remaining files. The case of the pawn on
the a or h files (or rook's pawn) is
easy to understand. In order to
keep alive the threat to play
a7–a8=Q (or h7–h8=Q), the
king defending the pawn goes to
the corner only after a check on
the file. If the queen stays on the
file it is stalemate. If she moves
from it her own king has *not*
moved and the other king emerges
from the corner to threaten
a7–a8=Q again. Remember, we
are assuming that the queen's own
consort is too far away to help
her.

The bishop's pawn on the
seventh rank draws under the
stated conditions because the supporting king can go to the corner
and the pawn cannot be captured
by the queen, as stalemate would
result. Again there is no time
available for approach moves by
the king partnering the queen.
For example White: Kg8 pf7;
Black: Kb3 Qf4. Play might proceed 1 ... Qg5+ 2 Kh8 Qf6+
3 Kg8 Qg6+ 4 Kh8 Q×f7 stalemate. The attack cannot be use-
fully varied because the queen
cannot find a square which controls f8, the queening square, and
also g8 and h8, one of which can
be occupied by the white king.

We conclude this section with
some exercises that show passed

pawns in play against pieces.

Exercise 19

White to play and win

Exercise 20

Black to play and win

Exercise 21

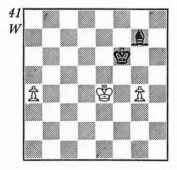

White to play and win. The critical point here is the bad position of the black king (*41*)

Exercise 22

White to play and draw

Exercise 23

Can White win?

E: STARTING A GAME; CASTLING AND SOME OTHER RULES

The Starting Position

In the first sections of this book we have described the various chess pieces and their functions. At the start of a game each piece has its appointed place. Diagram 44 shows the pieces at the start of a game.

Q-side   *K-side*

Q-side   *K-side*

The board is often divided, for descriptive purposes, into two halves, namely the king's and the queen's side, and the pieces on each side described accordingly. Thus the white pieces on a1, b1 and c1 are designated queen's rook, queen's knight and queen's bishop respectively, and similarly those on f1, g1 and h1 are the king's bishop, king's knight and king's rook. These descriptions have some value in the early stages of a game, but as the pieces move from side to side in the course of a game their value declines. However, the term has greater value when applied to the bishops—White's king's bishop moves on the white squares, while the queen's bishop plays only on the black. At a late stage of the game therefore the term king's or queen's bishop has a value as the bishop so described is immediately recognisable.

The distinction between K-side and Q-side pieces applies equally to Black, although it should be noted that the black king's and queen's bishops play on opposite coloured squares to their white counterparts.

Pawns normally bear the name of the piece in front of which they stand at the start of the game. We therefore have queen's rook pawn, queen's knight pawn etc.

It is a rule of the game that White always has the first move. White has a choice of twenty moves with which to start the game—sixteen pawn moves and four knight moves, and Black has a similar choice when replying. How White should commence the game and Black defend himself is the subject of further discussion in Chapter 4.

Castling

A special move by king and rook is permitted provided:

(a) that neither king nor rook have already moved in the game;

(b) that no pieces stand between king and rook;

(c) that the king does not pass over a square commanded by a hostile piece;

(d) that the king is not in check—castling out of check is not allowed.

Either the king's rook or the queen's rook may be used. In *both* cases the king moves two squares towards the rook which then jumps the king and lands on the next square beyond him. Diagram 45 shows the position after White has castled K-side and Black on the Q-side.

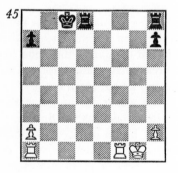

The move is symbolised by 0–0 for castling K-side and 0–0–0 for the Q-side. The terms castles *long*, or *short* are sometimes used and are self-explanatory.

Exercise 24

What castling moves are available to both White and Black? Would the answer be altered if there was a black pawn at c6?

Drawn Games

There are only two results to a game of chess. The first is checkmate. In practice players normally resign when mate is seen to be inevitable. The other is a drawn game. The several ways in which this can come about are discussed below.

A: *By Agreement*. This can be at any stage of the game, but should not be done until the position reached is one in which neither side has a reasonable chance of reaching a decisive result. It is to be regretted that many of the world's leading players do not set a good example in this respect. The most natural type of drawn position is one in which the reduction of material has made a win impossible.

B: *50 Move Rule.* To prevent an obdurate player going on and on in a drawn position in which his only hope of victory can be a blunder by his opponent, the above rule may be invoked. Either player may claim a draw if no capture has been made or pawn moved for 50 moves (by *both* players).

C: *Repetition of Position.* If exactly the same position occurs three times, either player may claim a draw. The correct procedure must be observed: a player who, by making his move, will bring about a threefold repetition of moves must claim the draw by demonstrating that it is his intention so to move and thereby claim the draw. Once he has moved the right to claim the draw is lost.

It will be seen that B and C between them form a formidable protection against an opponent who would otherwise play on endlessly.

D: *Perpetual Check.* A position may arise in which one side is able to go on checking indefinitely. In such a case, the game is drawn. Perpetual check is often the refuge of the weaker party in circumstances such that to stop checking would involve loss of the game. For example in diagram 47 White is the exchange and a pawn down. But he draws by a combination starting with a sacrifice of the queen.

Foguelman

Rossetto

1 Q×g6+ f×g6 2 Rg7+ Kh8 3 Rf7+ Kg8 4 Rg7+ and Black cannot avoid the checks and White cannot afford to stop them.
E: *Stalemate.* This has already been discussed (p. 7) and is mentioned here for the sake of completeness. Stalemate, like perpetual check, is one of the weapons of the defender. Thus in diagram 48:

White draws by 1 Qf2 since 1 ... Q×f2 is stalemate. Black

must capture otherwise he loses his queen.

Exercise 25

Black to play and draw

Chess Etiquette

Most beginners shift pieces tentatively in order to see better what the effects of the proposed move will be. They think that this is allowable so long as the piece or pawn is held in the hand. Such behaviour is quite natural and even excusable in the novice, but it is intolerable in all forms of competitive chess. The rule is that a piece or pawn, if touched, must be moved. All players should learn 'touch and move' as early as possible.

2 Some Tactical Manoeuvres

The purpose of this chapter is to discuss various tactical devices and the principles underlying them. These apply to most parts of the game and will be exemplified repeatedly in the next three chapters on the middle game, opening and end game. There is an element of strategy in tactics and of tactics in strategy. Recognising a broad distinction despite the dovetailing, we deal here in a preliminary manner with detailed operations, the possibility of which arises from the powers and functions of the chessmen. In the following chapters 3, 4 and 5 we are concerned with the strategy of the conduct of a game as a whole, or at some stage in its progress.

In general, advantage is gained by a well chosen threat, or series of threats, either against the king or some part of his forces. Such threats may follow an exchange and after a succession of them there may well be found a crack in the opponent's defences.

Gain or Loss of Material

The objective of a player is to checkmate the hostile king and this is often achieved by combination of pieces in the middle game. Nevertheless the majority of well-conducted games involve a struggle for mastery in which checkmate is postponed to an ending. The chief factors in such dominance are material and positional advantage. In other words, a player usually seeks the attrition of his opponent's forces and endeavours to place his pieces and pawns on the squares where they will be most effective both for attack and defence.

The Average Relative Values of the Chessmen

It is already clear to the reader that the queen, moving as she does in all directions, is by far the most valuable of the pieces. The rook comes next, because it can reach every square on the board and lacks only the power of diagonal motion. The bishop and knight are less powerful and pawns in action are the weakest, even though they may eventually be promoted. That is a potentiality, not a power.

Experience has shown that a queen is a little weaker than two rooks on the same rank or file, but if the rooks do not protect one another they may fall to some type of attack by the queen.

A rook is definitely stronger than a bishop or a knight, which are about equal in value. If a player can capture a rook while losing a bishop or knight, he is said to 'win the exchange'. Two bishops are stronger than a bishop and knight.

Circumstances affect all these and similar estimations. In many end games one knight is stronger than one bishop. Two bishops or a bishop and a knight are stronger than a rook. A bishop or a knight is approximately equal to three pawns.

These statements are based on results in practical play and can be summarised by the following numerical values: queen, 9; rook, 5; bishop or knight, 3; pawn, 1; some authorities prefer the value of 3.5 for bishop and knight. Two bishops are better than two knights in most positions. The reasons for this are instructive: the wide ranging mobility of a bishop gives it the advantage over

the short stepping knight, but the knight has the counter advantage that it is not restricted to squares of one colour. But two bishops eliminate this weakness as between them they cover all the squares on the board.

In view of this analysis, the value of 3.5 for bishop and 3 for knight is nearer the average value. Such figures must be used with great caution; they are only approximations. If positional factors need not be taken into account, they are good guides in the matter of exchanges.

Calculation of the outcome of exchanges is a simple matter from our present point of view, which is restricted to the material value of chessmen captured and recaptured by the enemy. Naturally the effect of exchanges needs to be carefully considered, but that topic is deferred (see *captures* below). It must be realised that loss of material, even loss of a pawn, is more often fatal than not, though many players do not have the necessary skill to exploit such an advantage. Loss of the exchange (rook for bishop or knight) is still more serious and loss of a piece leaves the weaker side with little prospect of a draw; it is therefore of the utmost importance to avoid loss of material and to attempt to gain it. Attack is said to be the best defence, but in chess it is often wise to ensure security before embarking on adventure. Therefore:

Before Each Move

Make it an absolute rule to note whether the last move of your opponent is an attack on one of your men by one of his of inferior value. Such an attack may be direct, or indirect by discovering a piece. In diagram 50 is seen a) one of the commonest forms of attack, in this case of a bishop by a pawn and b) we see attack by discovery.

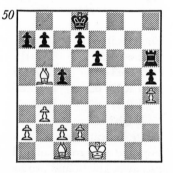

a) Black plays 1 . . . a6 and White must move his bishop on b5 (unless counterattack is sound, of which more anon). But he must not retreat to a4, because . . . b5 would then follow and the bishop is trapped and will fall to the pawn. This manoeuvre, incidentally, may be a little more complicated. In diagram 50 remove the pawn on b3 to b2. Then after 1 . . . a6 2 Ba4 b5 3 Bb3 c5 wins the bishop for a pawn.

b) White plays 1 d3 and this discovers an attack on the rook at h6 by the bishop on c1.

If an equal or superior piece attacks one of your units, make sure that the latter is adequately defended, or, if not, move it away from the attack.

Captures

Pieces that can be taken are said to be 'en prise' and the first rule of chess play is to note all such and to avoid loss of material by reason of chess blindness or easily avoidable blunders. As we are only considering the matter one move deep, this should present no real difficulty. Yet the fact is that the great majority of beginners are extremely careless and throw pieces and pawns away with prodigality. Admittedly it will take more time to learn how to anticipate dangers from sequences of moves but at least one ought to be able to suppress at an early stage a tendency to the most superficial blunder. As James Mason* once said, they could spoil the greatest chess genius that ever lived.

Consecutive Captures and Recaptures

It frequently happens that a plan

* Famous Irish-American-English player. USA Champion 1876-78.

is made to win material by concentrating attack on a piece or
pawn that is immovable for one
of several possible reasons. A very
simple case would be a pawn
blocked by a pawn of the other
side. Other examples are indicated in the sequel.

'To take or not to take'—that
is the question. To resolve this
dubiety, the first thing to note is
the number of attacking and
defending pieces. If the attacking
pieces outnumber the defending
pieces, even by one man, you may
proceed with the contemplated
scheme and will then win the
pawn or piece attacked. Suppose
this is a, defended by b, c, d, e and
your attack is by g, followed by
h, i, j, k then:

1 g×a	b×g
2 h×b	c×h
3 i×c	d×i
4 j×d	e×j
5 k×e	

If g etc. is our side we have
taken a, b, c, d, e and lost g, h,
i, j, a gain of one piece. There is
however a most important quali-
fication and that depends on the
order of support, in relation to the
values of the pieces. Remember
that the series can be broken at
will at any stage by either party.
Hence if there is a series of captures and recaptures available, it
is important to see that the pieces
will be removed in correct order.

This is obviously such that the
less valuable pieces will leave the
board first.

In diagram 51 White, to play,
can safely embark on capturing
the black pawn on d5.

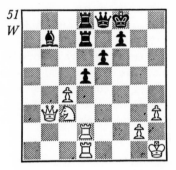

51
W

The possible moves would be:

1 c4×d5	e6×d5
2 Nc3×d5	Bb7×d5
3 Rd2×d5	Rd7×d5
4 Rd1×d5	Rd8×d5
5 Qb3×d5	

White has captured two pawns,
bishop and two rooks and Black
takes pawn, knight and two rooks.

But in diagram 52 where Q×d5
has to be played earlier, White,
though he has five attacking men
against the defence's four, can
only play 1 c4×d5 with safety.

If he proceeds 1 c×d5 exd5
2 N×d5 B×d5 he has lost knight
for pawn, and makes matters still
worse by 3 R×d5 R×d5 4 Q×d5
R×d5 5 R×d5 ... counting up,
we find that White has got only
rook and pawn for his queen and
will lose the game in consequence.

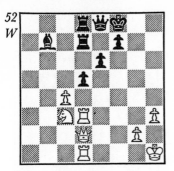

Exercise 26

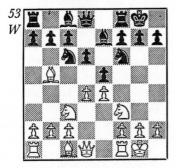

White to play and win a pawn

Exercise 27

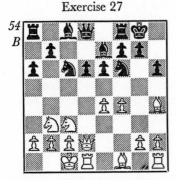

Can Black play 1 . . . N×e4 ?

The Pin

If a piece or pawn stands between an enemy piece and the homeside king, that is in the line of potential movement of the piece so that, except for the intervening piece or pawn, the king would be in check, then that piece or pawn is 'pinned' against the king. In this way a pawn, knight, bishop, rook or queen can be pinned. The piece which pins may be a bishop, rook or queen, but not a knight, or pawn for obvious reasons. There is no interposition against a check by a knight.

A pinned knight cannot move at all—the restriction is complete. Similarly, a bishop pinned by a rook is immovable and equally a rook pinned by a bishop. But a bishop pinned by a bishop or a rook pinned by a rook can move in the line of fire of the pinning piece and can, of course, capture it. It is for this reason that the former kind of pin (i.e. that of bishop on rook) is the most dangerous, as the pin cannot be lifted by the movement of the pinned piece and can only be broken by the king moving or assistance from other pieces. A pinned queen always has the resource of capturing the pinning piece, but it is usually of no avail since the resulting exchange is normally materially unfavourable.

It will be clear that 'pinning' is **an** important tactical device and can be used a) to immobilise a piece or pawn so that attacks can be concentrated upon it, and b) to gain material at once by a pin of a major piece such as rook or queen by one of less value. A common pin of the queen is by a rook and this operation will usually enable the game to be won. Examples of 'pins' are illustrated in diagram 55.

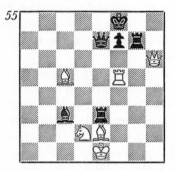

The white knight and bishop (e2) are pinned by the black bishop and rook (e3), whilst the black queen, pawn and rook (g7) are pinned by the white bishop (c5), rook and queen respectively.

It is, more often than not, wise to get rid of a pin at an early stage: a) by interposing a man in the line of the pin, b) by moving the king, or c) by driving away the pinning piece. If a queen is pinned by bishop or rook, the only resource is a) and the interposition must be between the queen and the pinning piece. If this is not possible, very serious loss will be sustained.

Defences against pins are illustrated in diagram 56.

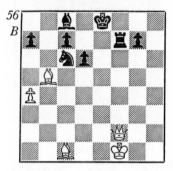

The knight on c6 is pinned by the bishop of b5 and is not defended, hence 1 B×c6+ is threatened. The alternative defences are . . . Bd7 (type *a* above), . . . Kd7 (type *b*), and, once the knight has been protected, the bishop can be driven away by . . . a6 (type *c*). It should be noted that only the first of these gets rid of the pin.

Black, in turn, pins the white queen on f2 by the rook on f7. This can be alleviated by interposing the bishop (c1) on f4. However, Black can reply . . . g5 winning the pinned bishop, which cannot escape from the pawn's attack except at the loss of his queen.

In making exchanges it is important to make sure that after the capture or captures a piece is not left liable to a pin involving later absolute or relative loss of material. An example is shown in diagram 57.

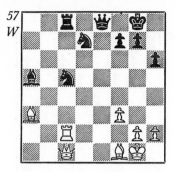

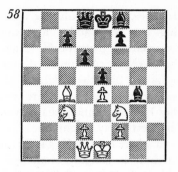

Here White might calculate that he can gain a knight by 1 B×c5 N×c5 2 R×c5 R×c5 3 Q×c5. But there follows 2 ... Bb6 and the rook is pinned and lost to the combined attack of rook and bishop.

There are many analogous situations and it goes without saying that one must not only guard against the danger in defence but also be alert to use the tactical device in attack. 'Pin and win' is a catchphrase often heard in the chess room. It is not as simple as that, but nevertheless pins do frequently give a winning advantage when properly applied and followed up.

Pins other than those against the King

These are not true pins but are often so called.

For example in diagram 58 the black bishop on g4 pins the knight f3 to the queen d1 (for the moment ignore the other pieces).

The fundamental difference from the true pin against a king is that the pseudo-pinned piece is perfectly free to move in any direction in accordance with its normal powers. The only reason for not doing so is the ensuing material loss caused, in this instance by ... B×d1. It may well happen that the pseudo-pinned piece can do adequate damage in moving and thus compensate for the loss of the queen. That must be attended to and time is gained enabling the queen to be moved out of danger. Worse still the queen might be able to capture the pinning piece if the latter is undefended.

A brilliant combination attributed to Philidor* illustrates a contemptuous treatment of a pseudo-pin. In diagram 58 (above) we have a position that sometimes occurs early in a game, but only the pieces relevant to the combination have been shown.

* Andre Danican Philidor, world's strongest player c1745-95.

However, as a punctilio the white king has been added and this necessitates a pawn on f2. (Exercise: Why?). As discussed, the bishop–g4 pins the knight at f3. But, with impunity, White can play 1 N×e5, winning that pawn. The best reply might be 1 ... d×e5 whereupon 2 Q×g4. But if the bait is greedily swallowed: 1 N×e5 B×d1 then 2 B×f7+ Ke7 3 Nd5 mate.

There follow four exercises showing the pin in various forms.

Exercise 30

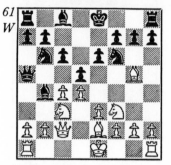

White plays 1 a3—how should Black reply?

Exercise 28

White to play and win

Exercise 31

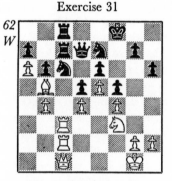

White to play and win

Exercise 29

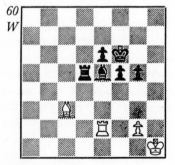

White to play and win

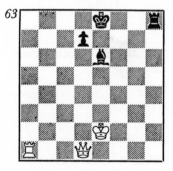

Gains of Material with Help of Checks

If a bishop, rook or queen can check the king and there is no practicable interposition in reply, the king must move aside. It may then happen that a piece originally beyond the king and in the line of fire can be captured.

Diagram 63 (p. 38) shows two cases of common occurrence.

a) White wins a rook by 1 Ra8+ Ke7 (or 1 ... Kf7) 2 R×h8.

b) Black wins the queen by 1 ... Bg4+ 2 K moves B×d1. Reminder —the queen is worth about three bishops. Hence 3 K×d1 is irrelevant.

Exercise 33

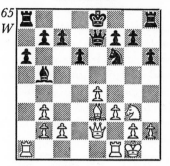

White to play

no time to attend to the attacked piece, which may then be captured with impunity.

Diagram 66 shows this idea implemented by rook and bishop.

Exercise 32

Can White win a pawn by 1 c×d5 e×d5 2 N×d5 ?

The Fork

The absolute priority of the king implies that, if a simultaneous attack can be made on the king *and* a hostile piece, it is the king that must be made safe. There is

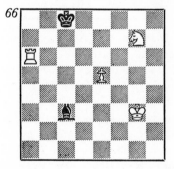

a) Rook—1 Rc6+ Kd7 2 R×c3.

b) Bishop—1 ... B×e5+ 2 K any B×g7.

These illustrate the fork even though the angle of the fork in the case of the rook is 180°, though the bishop's fork is only 90°.

But when we speak of forks we usually mean that which is the

peculiar privilege of the knight
and in which chess players find
particular satisfaction. In the
early stages this pleasing manoeuvre must be always kept in
mind, as quite a sizeable propor-
tion of games will be won and lost
thereby. A piece particularly
vulnerable to this tactic is the
queen's rook.

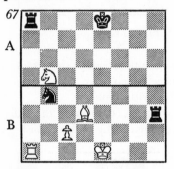

Diagram 67 (A) illustrates a
frequent occurrence. White to
play wins a rook by 1 Nc7+ (often
N×c7+)). 1 . . . K any 2 N×a8.

67 (B) shows the same combination for Black, but with the addition of a preparatory move:
1 . . . R×d3 2 c×d3 Nc2+ 3 K
moves N×a1. Here the net result
is the gain of a bishop. Sometimes
the forking knight can be captured after N×R. In such cases
the gain is of R for N. The win of
R for B or N is described as winning the exchange.

As this type of position can
easily be reached early in a game,
it is necessary to keep c7 (c2 for
White) under observation. At the
outset the queen performs this
function but she may be moved
away. A method that is often used
to avoid this particular danger is
castling.

The next two exercises show
the 'fork' winning games from
tournament chess.

Exercise 34

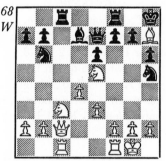

White to play and win

Exercise 35

Black to play and win

Double Attack and Virtual Double Attack without Check

Such situations may lead to decisive gains though the scope for

defence is clearly greater. One or other of the attacked pieces might institute some counter-attack. This matter, however, is interpolated here because it is so clearly related to the forks with checks. Perhaps the simplest fork is the attack of two rooks by a pawn. For example rooks on c6 and e6, pawn on d4. By playing d4–d5 White wins a rook for pawn.

The fork of two pieces by a knight is shown in diagram 70 (A) and the virtual attack of two pieces in diagram 70 (B).

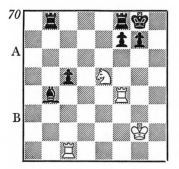

Other things being relatively unimportant (i.e. no serious counter-attack) 1 Nd7 and 1 . . . Bd2 will win the exchange.

Discovered Check and Double Check

The terms are self-explanatory. The checking piece does not move, but a piece of the same colour screening the hostile king

is moved, thus discovering a check. When the screening piece is moved, it can often do a great deal of damage.

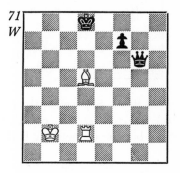

In diagram 71, 1 B×f7+ discovers check from the rook; the black king must move and then 2 B×g6, so that the damage inflicted by the screening piece extends over two moves.

If a check by discovery is threatened, it is almost always good play to avoid it by moving the king, by attack of the potential checker, or by interposition of a man in the line of fire.

A check by discovery can also in some cases be a double check (++), which is especially dangerous for the king because he *must* move. No capture or interposition is possible. Diagram 72 shows a checkmate preceded by double check.

White plays 1 Bb6++ Ke8 2 Rd8 mate. The queen on b4 has been introduced in order to show her helplessness against a

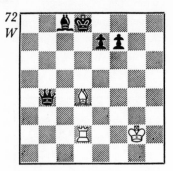

double check. She could take the checking rook *or* the checking bishop but she cannot take both.

Exercise 36

White to play and win

Exercise 37

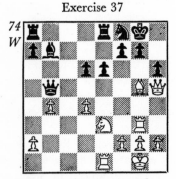

White to play and win

On Planning

The course of the game of chess should not consist of a series of unrelated moves. A good player coordinates the moves of his pieces so that they work together to achieve the maximum results. The position of a chess player is not dissimilar to that of a general in command of an army. The successful military commanders have always operated with a plan and purpose in mind; similarly in chess. A planless player will always be defeated by an opponent who sets out to achieve certain strategic objectives.

The difficulty that faces the beginner is the question: which plan? Naturally this will vary from position to position. The plan must be based on the individual characteristics of the position.

For example, the defences of the opposing king may be poorly organised. An attack on the king's position would be a logical corollary. If, on the other hand, the opposing king is well defended and our opponent could summon to the defence more pieces than could be mustered for the attack, it is probable that the attack would be unsuccessful. It may be helpful to return to the military analogy: good strategy does not consist in launching an attack against the best defended fortress on the opposing side until that position has been undermined and weakened by offensives elsewhere.

The plan may have to be varied according to the changing nature of the position. For example: we may have launched an attack on the opposing king. Our opponent may have the choice of two defences. First, by surrendering a pawn he could blunt the attack with many exchanges and transpose into the end game; secondly he might decide to hold on as best he could and see whether he could survive the attack. Our plan varies according to the defence. In the first case we would be a pawn up and our concern would be with the technical problems involved in evaluating the pawn advantage; in the second we would have to consider how to force our attack through our opponent's defences. The problems involved in either case are quite distinct.

Any plan must be in accordance with the tactical requirements of the position. It is no use planning a transition into a won ending and ignoring a direct attack on our queen. This latter threat must be attended to at once. But the strategical structure of the position influences the result of the tactics. To return to our military analogy for the last time—the outcome of fighting between two equally matched armies may be very difficult to forecast, but if one of the sides is fighting from the better terrain, has superior lines of communication, better placed artillery, then the result will not be long in doubt. A skilful general fights only when the military factors are in his favour, and so does a chess master.

The Elements

In the preceding section we have emphasised the necessity for a player to have a plan, albeit even a limited one. But the reader may ask: how do I know which plan to adopt? This depends upon the nature of the position which, in turn, is determined by the various elements that constitute its make-up. Probably the simplest and best approach to this problem is the analysis first published by Znosko–Borovsky in his well-known book *The Middle Game in Chess*. He argued that a position is made up of a combination of three elements—Force, Time and Space. What are these?

A: *Force*
This is obvious. The player with the greater number of pieces has the advantage over his opponent, i.e. the player with the greater force calls the tune. The reader will recall some of the end games in Chapter 1, where the small material advantage of a pawn in

many cases rendered the defender helpless.

B: *Time*

This is a little more difficult, but nevertheless fairly easy to understand. The best explanation is by example: after, say, ten moves of a game one player may have developed five of his pieces, while his opponent has only managed two. Clearly the first player has a superiority in that he could launch an attack with his five pieces which his opponent, with only two pieces available for the defence, would find it difficult to repel. The essential point to grasp about an advantage of time is that it is transitory—if the first player in the example above fails to exploit his superiority, then his opponent, by bringing his other pieces into play, equalises the game.

Two important corollaries follow this argument:
a) At the beginning of a game it is of prime importance to develop the pieces as quickly as possible.
b) If a player has an advantage in time, he must exploit it vigorously, lest it fade away.

C: *Space*

The hardest of the elements to understand, but it is very important. Once again the concept is best explained by an example.

White has a massive advantage

75

in space, based primarily on his chain of pawns and pieces a4, b4, c5, d4, e5, f6, g5, h6, that stretches across the board hemming Black into much less than his fair share of the board. The extra space at White's command gives him greater freedom to manoeuvre his pieces. This enables him to post his pieces on the best squares available and to change the target of his attack more quickly than his cramped opponent can manage to organise his defences.

How to exploit an advantage in the elements is discussed in the next chapter, The Middle Game.

In the four diagrams below (p. 45), the player with the move has an advantage in one of the elements. Which is it?

Exercise 38

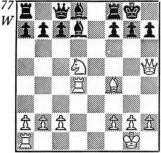

Exercise 40

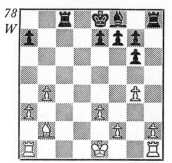

Exercise 39

Exercise 41

Nomenclature

So far in Chapters 1 and 2 the algebraic (coordinate) system has been employed. It is now time to learn the system of notation used in the UK, British Commonwealth and USA for recording games and other sequences of moves, or to describe the position of individual men, which will be used in Chapters 3, 4, 5 and 6.

Now, in contrast to the algebraic system, the notation adopted by English-speaking countries is different for White and for Black. In diagram 80 we see how the squares are described from the White side and in diagram 81 the inverted description looking down, as it were, from the Black side. In each case the files are denoted by letters representing the white and black pieces which stand on them at the beginning of a game.

Black

80

QR8	QN8	QB8	Q8	K8	KB8	KN8	KR8
QR7	QN7	QB7	Q7	K7	KB7	KN7	KR7
QR6	QN6	QB6	Q6	K6	KB6	KN6	KR6
QR5	QN5	QB5	Q5	K5	KB5	KN5	KR5
QR4	QN4	QB4	Q4	K4	KB4	KN4	KR4
QR3	QN3	QB3	Q3	K3	KB3	KN3	KR3
QR2	QN2	QB2	Q2	K2	KB2	KN2	KR2
QR1	QN1	QB1	Q1	K1	KB1	KN1	KR1

White

White

81

KR8	KN8	KB8	K8	Q8	QB8	QN8	QR8
KR7	KN7	KB7	K7	Q7	QB7	QN7	QR7
KR6	KN6	KB6	K6	Q6	QB6	QN6	QR6
KR5	KN5	KB5	K5	Q5	QB5	QN5	QR5
KR4	KN4	KB4	K4	Q4	QB4	QN4	QR4
KR3	KN3	KB3	K3	Q3	QB3	QN3	QR3
KR2	KN2	KB2	K2	Q2	QB2	QN2	QR2
KR1	KN1	KB1	K1	Q1	QB1	QN1	QR1

Black

On White's side the files from left to right are QR (queen's rook's file), QN (queen's knight's file), QB (queen's bishop's file), Q (queen's file), K (king's file) and then KB, KN and KR files. The ranks are numbered 1 to 8 from the white base line to the black base line.

Thus a1 is QR1, c4 is QB4, e3 is K3, g6 is KN6 and h8 is KR8. From the black side the files are denoted by the same letters as from the white side.

From the black side the ranks

are numbered from the black base line, which is 1, to the white base line, which is Black's eighth rank.

Thus a1 is QR8, c4 is QB5, e3 is K6, g6 is KN3 and h8 is KR1 for Black's men.

It should be noted that, in this system, capital letters are used to denote all pieces and pawns of either colour. In addition the piece and the square are separated by a hyphen, and the symbol 'P' is used.

In order to avoid ambiguity, it may be necessary to specify a particular square on which a capture is made. In that case we use the symbol appropriate for the capturing man and not that correct for the captured man. If there is ambiguity arising from the possibility of two similar pieces making the move, it will usually suffice to add the rank number of the piece moved. In other cases it may be necessary to specify the square of origin exactly. Thus if we had white R's at e7 and e2 and a black P at e5 and the move was R(e7)×P, it would be sufficient to write R7×P. But if White had N's at b2 and d2 and the move was N(b2)×P(e4), the correct symbol would be NN2×P, because N2×P would be ambiguous.

As illustration we give a short game set down in both systems. The game was played in Paris in 1858. The player with the white pieces was the famous master Morphy, his opponent two consulting amateur players.

1 P–K4 P–K4	e4 e5	
2 N–KB3 P–Q3	Nf3 d6	
3 P–Q4 B–N5	d4 Bg4	
4 P×P B×N	d×e5 B×f3	
5 Q×B P×P	Q×f3 d×e5	
6 B–QB4 N–KB3	Bc4 Nf6	
7 Q–QN3 Q–K2	Qb3 Qe7	
8 N–B3 P–B3	Nc3 c6	
9 B–KN5 P–N4	Bg5 b5	
10 N×P P×N	N×b5 c×b5	
11 B×NP+ QN–Q2	B×b5+ Nbd7	
12 0–0–0 R–Q1	0–0–0 Rd8	
13 R×N R×R	R×d7 R×d7	
14 R–Q1 Q–K3	Rd1 Qe6	
15 B×R+ N×B	B×d7+ N×d7	
16 Q–N8+ N×Q	Qb8+ N×b8	
17 R–Q8 mate	Rd8 mate	

This game is perhaps the most famous example of the exploitation of an advantage of time. The position arising after Black's 12th move was discussed in detail in exercise 28.

3 The Middle Game

Introduction

For purposes of exposition, chess writers usually divide the game into three parts: namely, opening, middle game and end game, and we shall follow this practice.

a) *The Opening.* This phase of the game covers, on average, perhaps the first fifteen moves of play, and is concerned with the placing of the pieces and pawns in what are deemed to be the best positions for attack and defence. This implies what is termed development of the pieces. On average it might take about fifteen moves of play on both sides, but such an estimate is an approximation, since some developments are quicker than others. Once this has been achieved, we reach

b) *The Middle Game.* During this stage, which dovetails with the opening, the developed pieces of both sides struggle for advantage. Many games never proceed further than the middle game, as one of the players obtains a decisive advantage, but those that do eventually reach

c) *The Ending.* If the position after the opening is level, or if one player has only a small advantage (e.g. an extra pawn) over his opponent, it is unlikely that either will be able to force a decision during the middle game. As the pieces are exchanged during the course of play, the players will reach the end game. It is difficult to state where the middle game finishes and the end game begins, just as it is equally difficult to define the transition point between the opening and middle game. However, the end game is normally considered to start when the forces are reduced to one or two pieces on either side, with supporting pawns, and the problems concerned are mainly technical. It is during this stage that the player with a small plus will seek to convert it into a winning advantage.

The opening and the end game are conducted in accord with recognised principles and are thus profitably studied at an early stage. These are the parts of the game for which the appropriate chess theory is most advanced. Indeed, over the years, the theory of the opening has evolved continuously and some general maxims have emerged.

Similarly, in the end game certain positions and combinations of pieces constantly recur and the more important of these should be memorised so that the standard wins and draws can be immediately recognised and used if desired. For example, a few of the principles of king and pawn versus king were examined in Chapter 1; these are of fundamental importance.

The problems of classification and analysis are much more difficult in the middle game. Probably every game has some unique feature and this applies with particular force to the middle game. The enormous variety of positions that can arise are difficult to categorise. It is therefore necessary to generalise and try to indicate the problems and tactical features which are most worthy of attention. There is no substitute for practice over the board, if mastery of the middle game is to be achieved.

Reference is regularly made to chapter 6 during the next three chapters, where points discussed in the text are further amplified in the Games Section. The text is complete in itself, and the reader in a hurry may if he wishes leave the references for study at a later date. However, a deeper appreciation will be gained if the references are followed up as they are reached.

Exploitation of Material Advantages

For purposes of exposition we are considering each of the elements in isolation. In practice, however, all relevant pieces should be considered together and the relationships can be very complex. For example, a player's advantage in time may be offset by his opponent's superior material, qualitatively or quantitatively. The problems raised by this kind of balance account for much of the fascination of chess. However, for the moment, let us assume that a player, all other things being equal, has won a material advantage. How should he proceed?

If the advantage is very great (say a rook), a player can simply force his way through his opponent's defences and impose mate. But normally this cannot be done and progress must be carefully made step by step.

The obvious weapon of the superior party is simplification by level exchange.

The reason is clearly that x/y is greater than x+z/y+z. E.g. $4/2=2$ but $4+1/2+1=5/3=1\frac{2}{3}$. The one *caveat* is that the reduction of force must not be carried so far that what is left is insufficient to force a win under any circumstances. E.g. 2 N's+P v. N+P. We can exchange knight for knight with advantage to the stronger side, but not P for P, as 2 N's v. N is a draw.

Imagine that almost all the pieces have been removed, leaving only the kings, pawns and, say, White with an extra knight. White then wins easily by systematically attacking the black pawns with his king and knight and Black, with only his king, cannot prevent the double attack capturing his pawns. Ultimately, White will queen one of his additional pawns and force mate. Of course this assumes that there is no tactical breakthrough available to the weaker side. This occurs by pushing on pawns, with possible sacrifice of one or more of them in order to clear the way for promotion of another pawn.

If the material advantage is one of smaller degree, e.g. the exchange (R for N or B), the procedure must be slightly different. The player must use the superior power of his forces to progressively weaken, attack and finally capture his opponent's pawns. The following game is a classic example of the way to exploit the advantage of the exchange.

In the diagrammed position,

Schlechter

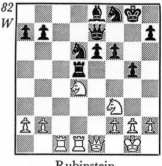

Rubinstein

White has won the exchange but Black has a solid position and an extra pawn and hence White's task is by no means an easy one. So he must proceed methodically. First he exchanges Black's rook for one of his own.

1 N–K2   B–B3

Schlechter defends himself as well as possible and attempts to build a strong position in the middle of the board. If Black avoids the exchange, White wins more easily through his control of both open lines, e.g. 1 ... R–N4 2 Q–Q2 N–K5 3 Q–K3 N–B4 (otherwise 4 Q×RP) 4 Q–R3 P–QR3 5 N2–Q4, and Black loses further material—if 5 ... R–N3 6 Q×N.

2 R×R   B×R
3 N3–Q4   P–K4

Or 3 ... B×RP 4 Q–R5 B–Q4 5 Q×P

4 N–QB3

A good move, forcing the exchange of the bishop—if 4 ...

B–B2 5 N(4)–N5 and Black must exchange knights or lose his QRP.

4 ...	Q–KB2
5 N×B	Q×N
6 N–N3	P–N3
7 R–Q1	Q–B3
8 Q–B3!	

Forcing the exchange of queens, for if 8 ... Q–Q2 (the only way to protect the knight), then 9 Q–Q3 and the pin on the knight wins a piece. Now White has reached the end game, but Rubinstein's winning procedure is so instructive that we give the remainder of the game.

8 ...	Q×Q
9 P×Q	N–K5
10 P–QB4	K–B2
11 R–Q8	

The rook now roams the board and there is nothing Black can do about it.

11 ...	K–K2
12 R–R8	P–QR4
13 P–B3	N–B6
14 P–B5	P×P
15 N×BP	N×P
16 R–R7+	

This little move is typical of a master's technique. The obvious 16 R×P is not so good; White interpolates a check that drives back Black's king, for if 16 ... K–Q3 17 N–K4+ K–K3 18 R×QRP N–N5 19 R–R4 N–Q4 20 R–R6+ K–K2 21 R–Q6 N–B2 22 R×P and wins easily.

16 ...	K–K1
17 K–B2	N–N5

18 R×QRP	K–B2
19 K–K3	P–R4
20 K–K4	

White brings his king into play —an essential technique in the end game.

20 ...	N–B3
21 R–R6	N–K2
22 P–N4!	

Fixing Black's pawns for attack

22 ...	P×P
23 P×P	K–N3
24 R–R7	K–B2
25 N–N7	K–N3
26 N–Q6	N–B3
27 R–QB7	N–Q5
28 N–B5	

Forcing a further exchange owing to the threat of 29 R–KN7 mate. In the sequel Black's knight is helpless against the superior powers of the rook.

28 ...	N×N
29 P×N+	K–R3
30 K–B3	N–R2
31 K–N4	P–K5
32 R–K7	P–K6
33 R×P	K–N2
34 R–K7+	1–0*

If 34 ... K–R3 35 R–KB7 and Black loses his knight and if 34 ... K–N1 35 K–R5 N–B1 36 K–R6 and the knight is lost next move. Rubinstein's careful play makes this game an ideal model that should be studied in detail.

The exploitation of an extra pawn is often more difficult

*This abbreviation is commonly used: see list of symbols.

(unless there is an immediate chance of queening the pawn) and by and large the player with the pawn should not rely upon it as an immediately decisive advantage. It is his opponent who has the problems! If the position is otherwise even, the end game will eventually be reached and the extra pawn will then usually constitute a decisive advantage. Therefore, the inferior party will endeavour to swing the game in his favour during the middle game by tactical combination and his opponent will be occupied repelling the threats. It should be realised that the loss of a pawn may open up lines for the pieces as in many gambits (see p. 71).

In the following example Black has won two pawns during the early stages of the game—however, as they are doubled, the advantage is not as great as it might have been.

Keres

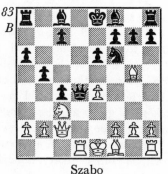

Szabo

White's only compensation is a slight lead in development, but it is inadequate. Black's immediate problem is to attend to the attack on his queen.

| **1 ...** | **Q–B4** |

The attack on the bishop gains time.

2 B–K3	**Q–B3**
3 B–K2	**B–N2**
4 B–B3	**P–K4**

A good move with a dual purpose: first it prevents White's threat of 5 P–K5 and, second, it blocks the position, preventing White from exploiting his lead in development.

5 0–0	**B–B4**
6 N–Q5	**B×B**
7 N×B	**0–0**
8 P–KN4	

Now that Black has completed his development satisfactorily, White's prospects are bleak. So he starts a rather wild attack with little prospect of success, since Black's position is quite sound. In the sequel it will be noted how carefully Black defends himself before endeavouring to use his extra pawns. Not, for instance 8 ... N×KP 9 N–B5 threatening N–K7+ and KR–K1 winning material.

| **8 ...** | **KR–K1** |
| **9 N–B5** | **N–Q2** |

Heading for a dominating position on Q6 (via QB4). This forces White to undertake an attack on the advanced pawn on QB5. Black's reply is quite adequate, since if 11 P×P N×P and the knight is well posted.

10 P–N3	**N–N3**
11 Q–B1	**P×P**

Forcing the exchange of queens —if 12 Q–N5 Q–N3 etc., and if White exchanges then 12 Q×Q B×Q 13 R–B1 N–B5 14 P×P N–Q7 15 R×B N×B+ 16 K–N2 N–Q7 followed by ... N×NP winning easily with the connected passed pawns.

12 P×P	**Q×Q**
13 R×Q	**QR–B1**
14 KR–Q1	**P–N3**
15 N–R6+	**K–N2**
16 P–N5	**P–QB4**
17 B–N4	**R–B2**
18 R–Q6	**N–B1**
19 R–KB6	**B×P**

White has sacrificed another pawn in order to gain the semblance of an attack and while this will be sufficient to recover a pawn, the black QBP wins the game for him.

20 R–Q1	**P–B5**
21 P×P	**P×P**
22 P–B3	**B–Q6**
23 R×RP	**N–K2**
24 R–Q6	**N–N1**
25 R–QB1	**R–N2**
26 B–Q7	**R–Q1**

Forcing another exchange— White's attack is obviously not getting anywhere.

27 N×N	**K×N**
28 B–B6	**R×R**
29 B×R	**R–N3**
30 B–Q5	**K–B1**

31 R–R1	**P–B6**
32 R–R8+	**K–K2**
0–1	

White resigned, as the advanced QBP will cost him a piece. A good example of the methodical technique required in positions of this type.

Advantage in Time

As discussed earlier, an advantage in time is essentially fugitive and must be exploited vigorously. In many ways it is akin to an advantage in material, but localised in one part of the board. The other player has equal material at his command, but it is all in the wrong part of the board—often not developed from their initial squares.

In the following example (diagram 84) White has played the opening badly and has already lost time. In the sequel his play is also weak and he loses even more, with drastic consequences.

Morphy

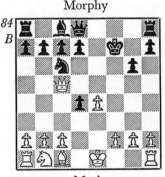

Meek

1 ...   **P–Q3**

Gaining more time by attacking the white queen.

2 Q–QN5   **R–K1**

3 Q–N3+

He should castle; he cannot afford to move his queen again.

3 ...   **P–Q4**

4 P–KB3   **N–R4**

5 Q–Q3   **P×P**

6 P×P   **Q–R5+**

7 P–KN3   **R×P+**

White's position is collapsing.

8 K–B2   **Q–K2**

9 N–Q2

A belated attempt by White to use pieces other than his queen, but it gives Morphy the chance to force the position by combinative play. Both kings are stationed on their KB2 square, but whereas White's king is soon to succumb to a mating attack, Black's is quite safe. Given time, White could develop his pieces, e.g. by R–KB1 K–N1 N–KB3 etc., but, and this is the essence of exploiting an advantage in time, Morphy gives him no time.

9 ...   **R–K6**

10 Q–N5

He cannot play 10 Q×QP because of 10 ... R–K7+ 11 K–N1 R–K8+ 12 K–N2 Q–K7+ 13 Q–B2 B–R6+ 14 K×B Q×Q. In the sequel White endeavours to defend K2(e2) with his queen.

10 ...   **P–B3**

11 Q–B1   **B–R6**

Another piece comes into play,

since if 12 Q×B R–K7+ wins, e.g. 13 K–N1 R–K8+ 14 N–B1 Q–K6+ 15 K–N2 R–K7 mate.

12 Q–Q1   **R–KB1**

Bringing his last piece into play with decisive results.

13 N–B3   **K–K1**

0–1

Resigned—if 14 B×R Q×B mate. The two white rooks played no part in the game. Black's rapid victory was due to his superior development (i.e. an advantage in time) and the fact that with an open board (no pawns on the K– or KB–files) he was able to develop irresistible threats against his opponent's king.

In the next example (diagram 85) it is White who has the advantage in time, but he needs to sacrifice a piece to break through his opponent's defences and gain the open lines necessary for his attack.

Flamberg

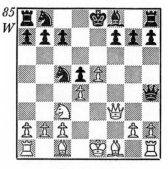

Spielmann

White is in check. He can interpose his queen but after 1 Q–B2 Q×Q+ 2 K×Q N–K3 3 N×P P–QB3 and ... N×P the game would be equal. Spielmann prefers to sacrifice two pawns (material) for an advantage in development (time).

1 P–KN3	Q×QP
2 B–K3	Q×P
3 0–0–0	P–QB3

White has lost two pawns, but has developed nearly all his pieces. His immediate threat was 4 R×QP so Black attempts to erect a pawn barrier against White's pieces.

4 N×P

But White sacrifices a piece to smash through Black's defences. Black's undeveloped position collapses rapidly.

| 4 ... | P×N |
| 5 R×P | Q–K3 |

Or 5 ... Q–K5 6 B–QN5+ N–B3 7 B3×N Q×Q 8 R–K1+ B–K2 9 R×B+ K–B1 10 R–K3+ and wins.

6 B–QB4!

Bringing another piece into play, threatening 7 R×N. This move is much stronger than 6 B×N B×B 7 R×B 0–0 and Black has avoided the worst.

| 6 ... | Q–K5 |
| 7 B×N! | 1–0 |

After 7 ... Q×Q 8 R–K1+ B–K2 9 R×B+ K–B1 10 R–Q8 mate. A drastic defeat: it is noticeable that once again the losing side has not developed his two rooks.

The temporary nature of an advantage in time can be vividly illustrated by the position after Black's third move: if Black could have an additional two developing moves, say, N–Q2–KB3 or ... B–K2 and ... 0–0, White would have no compensation for his sacrificed pawns and should lose the game. Therefore, White had to play energetically to exploit his temporary advantage. Games nos. 2 and 8 show great masters exploiting an advantage in time. Their opponents never gain a moment's rest. Game no. 8 is instructive as White loses time not in the opening, but in the middle game.

Advantage in Space

The player with the greater space at his command can move his pieces about the board with greater ease than his opponent. This factor alone can be a decisive advantage. Diagram 75 (p. 44), which was from the game Schlechter—John, Bremen 1905, shows a position in which White has a big advantage in space.

Schlechter won as follows:

1 R3–KB3

Threatening 2 N×B R×R 3 R×R R×N 4 R–B8+ K–N2 5 R–N8 mate. So Black must exchange.

1 ...	N×N
2 R×N	R×R
3 KP×R	R–K1
4 N–B7+	K–N1
5 N–K5	R–Q1

By recapturing with his king's pawn, white has made a dominating square available for his knight.

6 K–N2

Before breaking through, White improves his position as far as possible—an important procedure in this kind of situation.

6 ...	K–B1
7 P–R4	B–K1

To defend against a break-through based on P–KR5.

8 K–B3	B–B2
9 K–B4	K–K1
10 R–QN1	K–B1
11 P–N5	1–0

Black, an experienced master, realising the hopeless nature of his position, resigned. The continuation might have been 11 ... RP×P 12 P×P B–K1 13 P×P B×P 14 N×B P×N 15 K–K5 and Black cannot prevent the capture of his pawns; e.g. 15 ... R–K1 16 R–N7 K–N1 17 P–B7+ Black is completely move-bound.

A drastic example. However, in diagram 75, Black was already in a cramped position and was unable to prevent the systematic invasion by the white pieces.

In the next example White's task is far harder, as Black's position is less cramped and White has to take considerable

care to prevent Black from freeing his game (diagram 86).

Mikenas

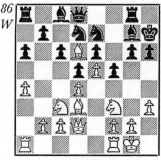

Alekhine

White's first move is symptomatic of his treatment of the position—he prevents Black's liberating move ... P–KN4.

1 P–KR4!	P–N3
2 N–K2	N–B1
3 P–QR5!	

White weakens the black squares in his opponent's position before undertaking any decisive action.

3 ...	P–QN4
4 P–KN3!	

An important prophylactic move. Black's only counterplay consists in ... P–KN4. Before undertaking a breakthrough on the Q-side White rearranges his king's defences so that the advance ... P–KN4 would be to his benefit.

4 ...	R–R1
5 K–N2	K–N1

6 R–R1   K–B2

Now ... P–KN4 would only open the KR–file to White's benefit—as Black's next move admits.

7 N–B4   R–KN1

8 P–N3

White intends to play P–QB4 and open a file on the Q-side. Black is unable to reorganise his pieces to meet this threat due to the limited space at his command.

8 ...   N–R2

9 P–B4   B–Q2

10 QR–QB1   B–KB1

11 B–K2!

Releasing the Q3 square for his knight and preventing 11 ... P–KN4 because of the variation 12 RP×P N×P 13 N×N+ P×N (or 13 ... R×N 14 N–R3 15 B–R5+ and wins) 14 B–R5+ K–N2 15 N×KP+! B×N 16 Q×P+ and mate follows.

11 ...   N–B1

12 P×QP   BP×P

13 B×B   N×B

Now the inferior nature of Black's position can be seen more clearly. As in the last example he cannot prevent the systematic infiltration of White's pieces.

14 R–B5   N–QR2

15 N–Q3   K–N2

16 R1–QB1   R–B1

17 R×R   B×R

If Black could manoeuvre his rook to QB1 he might have chances of defence, but he is so cramped that this is impossible.

18 Q–B3   K–R2

19 Q–B5   R–N2

20 Q–N6   Q–K2

Not 20 ... Q×Q 21 P×Q and the knight (a7) is lost.

21 N–B5   P–N4

A desperate counter-attack, as the position on the Q–side was rapidly becoming untenable.

22 P×P   P×P

23 N–K1!

A fine defensive move. If now 23 ... P–B5 24 B–N4 and if 23 ... P–KN5 24 N1–Q3 followed by N–B4.

23 ...   N–N3

24 N1–Q3   P–B5

25 R–KR1+   K–N1

26 B–N4   P×P

27 P×P

Black's attack has proved a fiasco, as his opponent's pieces have invaded the K–side. His position is now hopeless, as he must lose his KP or his QRP. The contrast between White's well placed pieces and Black's misplaced forces is a direct result of White's superiority in space. Black tried an ineffectual sacrifice, but resigned after:

27 ...   N–R5+

28 P×N   P×P

29 N–B2   R–B2

30 N×KP   K–R2

31 Q–Q6   1–0

The rules for exploiting a spatial advantage may be summarised as follows:

1: Unnecessary exchanges should

be avoided—the more pieces on the board, the greater will be the difficulties of the cramped player.

2: Careful attention should be given to an opponent's freeing moves, and these should be prevented if possible.

3: Before breaking into his opponent's position a player should strengthen his own defences to any necessary extent.

Game no. 4 is a famous example of the creation and exploitation of a spacial advantage.

The Centre

The chess board is divided into 64 squares, but the symmetrical relations of the empty board are disturbed by the placement of the pieces, particularly the king and queen. As in military strategy, it is found by experience that occupation of the centre may confer decisive advantages. Chess-wise this arises from the simple fact that a piece placed in the middle of the board controls far more squares than it would at the side of the board, e.g. a knight on d5 can move to eight squares, if placed on, say b2 it can move to only four squares, or again, a bishop on e4 can be played to thirteen squares, but on a1 to only seven squares.

The importance of the centre was recognised early in the development of chess theory. But how a player should set about controlling the centre has always been a matter of contention. The classical school argued that a successful occupation of the centre should be by pawns. This view was challenged by the so-called hypermodern school, who demonstrated that a pawn centre was not necessarily best, indeed in some instances it is weak, and that the centre was best occupied by pieces. But this view was found by experience to be too extreme. Neither of these ideas is correct, if taken by itself; a more opportunist strategy gives better results. This means that play is determined after consideration of the opponent's moves, rather than in a preconceived plan. It is essential to be ready to make a *safe*, relatively unchallengeable, occupation of the centre. In the French Defence: 1 P–K4 P–K3 2 P–Q4 P–Q4 3 P–K5, a superficial estimate is that White has *safely* occupied e5 with a supported pawn. But Black hits at the support by 3 ... P–QB4. Play continues either by direct attack on the centre or with a background potentiality of such attack. Right or wrong, Black has been presented with a clear objective and this is hardly what White set out to achieve. To put it another way, if the above 3 P–K5 could be shown to confer advantage, then Black's 2 ... P–Q4 is inadequate and, if no better move could be found, the French Defence would die of neglect. But this has not happened, nor does it seem likely to happen and the conclusion must be that 3P–K5 is premature.

The centre may be occupied by pawns or by pieces, or, and this is most common, by a combination of pawns and pieces. Modern theory has gone further and has shown that a player may allow his opponent a large centre provided he has adequate opportunities of counter-attack upon it.

We give two examples. In the first, White has complete control of the centre and Black is unable to prevent White building up a decisive attack. The second game shows the rôles reversed: Black is able to break up White's pawn centre and occupy the middle of the board with his pieces.

In diagram 87 White has a strong centre. Firstly, he marshals his pieces behind it.

Smyslov

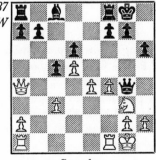

87
W

Spassky

1 Q–B2

An important move, recentralising the queen and preventing Black's only counter-attack on the centre by . . . P–KB4.

  1 . . .   **P–KR4**

2 R–B2

So as to retreat the knight to KB1 after . . . P–R5.

  2 . . .   **P–QN4**

Black attempts to gain play on the flanks. This is unsuccessful, as White's grip on the central squares is undisturbed.

  3 P–K5   **P–R5**

  4 N–B1   **B–B4**

  5 Q–Q2   **P×P**

  6 P×P

White threatens 7 N–K3, winning a piece.

  6 . . .   **B–N3**

  7 R–K1   **P–R6**

  8 P–Q6   **B–K5**

  9 N–K3   **Q–K3**

  10 R–B4   **B×P**

Now White's position is highly centralised behind the pawns on K5 and Q6. With startling rapidity White builds up a decisive attack on the black king. The advanced white centre prevents Black from coordinating his forces in the defence of his king; in particular, his rooks are inactive. It should be noted that the attack on the white king by the black bishop on g2 and pawn on h3 would be extremely dangerous for that monarch, if it could be supported by the black pieces. But centralised white forces not only prevent Black's pieces from assisting their colleagues but are also capable of launching a decisive attack on the black king at the same time.

11 N–B5

Threatening 12 N–K7+ K–R1 13 R–KR4 mate.

11 ...   KR–K1

12 R–K3

Bringing his extra piece into the attack with decisive effect.

12 ...   QR–Q1

13 N×P!

The combinative finish to White's strategy. If now 13 ... K×N 14 R–N3+ K–B1 15 R× BP+ Q×R 16 Q–R6+ and mate next move; or if 14 ... Q–N3 15 R×BP+ K×R 16 Q–B4+ K–N2 17 Q–B6+ and mate in two.

13 ...   R×P

14 N×Q   1–0

For, if 14 ... R×Q 15 R–N3+ K–R2 16 R–KR4 mate.

An impressive example of the power of centralised pieces and pawns. Spassky was only sixteen years old when he played this game.

In our next example White is not so successful (diagram 88).

In this position arising from the King's Indian Defence White has established a strong pawn centre. Black must attack this as quickly as possible. If he fails to do so he rapidly gets a bad game, e.g.

Euwe

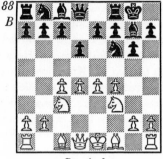

Sämisch

1 ... B–N5   2 B–K2   N–B3 3 P–Q5 N–N1   4 0–0 QN–Q2 5 N–KN5 B×B   6 Q×B P–KR3 7 N–B3 P–K3   8 P–K5 with the better game, Alekhine–Marshall, New York 1924.

1 ...   P–B4

2 P–Q5

Trying to maintain the pawns. 2 P×P Q–R4 (threat ... N×KP) 3 B–Q2 Q×BP with adequate play for Black.

2 ...   P–K3

3 B–Q3   P×P

4 BP×P

Or 4 KP×P R–K1+ and Black's pressure on the K-file secures equality.

4 ...   Q–N3

Posing White a problem; if 5 0–0 P–B5+ wins the bishop (d3).

5 N–Q2?

A plausible move, intending 6 N–B4 and 0–0, but he does not have time for this. White's correct reply is 5 Q–N3.

5 ...   N–N5

6 N–B4   Q–Q1

Again White discovers that he cannot castle because of . . . B–Q5+ and . . . N–B7+ winning the exchange. Nor can the offending knight be driven away by P–KR3 because of . . . Q–R5+. Black also threatens . . . P–B4, opening White's exposed king position.

7 B–K2   P–KR4
8 N–N5?

White's best is 8 B×N B×B 9 Q–B2 Q–R5+ 10 P–KN3 Q–K2 11 0–0 P–R5! and Black has a strong attack (White is weak on the light squares). As played he loses a piece.

8 . . .	**P–R3**
9 N5×P	**P–QN4**
10 N×B	**P×N**
11 P–K5	**Q×N**
12 P–KR3	**N–R3**
13 P–KN4	**N–Q2**
14 P×P	**Q–Q1!**

The White pawns look strong but they are unsupported by their undeveloped pieces and are actually very weak. Black has no difficulty in mounting an attack on the king.

15 0–0	**Q–R5**
16 R–B3	**P×P**
17 R–B3	**QR–K1**
18 B–Q2	**N×P**

An instructive moment. Black returns the piece in order to take control of the centre with his pieces.

19 P×N	**R×P**

20 B–K1	**Q–K2**
21 P–Q6	**Q–K3**

Black's queen, rook and bishop have dominating positions.

22 B–B1	**R–N4+**
23 R–KN3	**Q–K6+**

Taking advantage of the pinned rook.

24 K–N2	**B–Q5**
25 R×R+	**Q×R+**
26 0–1	

After 26 K–R1 Q–N8 is mate, and if 26 B–N3 N–B4 27 Q–B3 P–R5 wins easily. Nothing is left of White's once proud centre. A game of some historical importance, as up to that time White's centre was considered to be so powerful that Black's opening play was condemned as unsound. White can in fact do better than in the game, but nonetheless Black can obtain adequate counterplay.

The centre features one way or another in every master game. Therefore, all the games given in chapter 6 are relevant to some extent. Games 4 and 7 consider the French Defence pawn formation discussed above. Game no. 7 was of crucial importance in the development of chess theory. Coming to modern times Games 12 and 13 are very instructive. In the first White establishes a big centre which Black brilliantly undermines, whilst in the second White consolidates a similar centre and goes on to win.

The Pieces and their Characteristics in Middle Game Play

a) *The King*

The king is the most important of all the pieces for the fundamental reason that the capture of the king is the purpose of the game. Therefore the safety of the king is of paramount importance. By far the most common method of ensuring this is to castle, normally at an early stage of the game. As an illustration of the terrible things that can befall an uncastled king we would refer the reader to diagrams 84 and 85.

Therefore, in the early stages of a game, while there are many pieces, particularly the queens, on the board, the king is normally best placed at the side of the board, sheltered preferably by a shield of pawns.

It was Steinitz who first propounded the view that the king was a strong piece. The more pieces that are exchanged, the more the king can venture forth to take a hand in the fight. Indeed, in the end game, it is essential to bring the king into action both for offence and defence. Examples of the use of the king in the end game are given in Chapter 5.

But in the earlier part of the game the king is a weak piece that needs protection and this must on no account be neglected.

b) *The Queen*

The position of the queen is very similar to that of a battleship in naval warfare. By far the most powerful of the pieces, she has an immense capacity for destruction, combined with a susceptibility to attack from weaker units. In the early stages of the game the queen should not be developed in front of her pieces, as she will be liable to frequent attacks from minor pieces and pawns in face of which she will have to retreat, with loss of time (see Meek–Morphy, diagram 84). She should therefore be posted in a modest position on the second or third ranks, e.g. QB2, K2, or perhaps QN3. But once the queen can come into play, her enormous force can be devastating to the opposition, as in diagram 89.

Bernstein

89
W

Marshall

Materially the game is about equal, as Black will win either the knight or bishop by reason of the pawn fork on the two pieces. But White's queen now takes a decisive hand in the proceedings.

1 Q–B7	P–QN3
2 B–B4	P×N
3 B×P	

White has given back the piece in such a way that he now has an attack on Black's KN2. Marshall, in his notes to the game writes: 'The final moves now illustrate the tremendous power of the queen against unorganised forces'.

3 ...	R–B2
4 Q–N8+	R–B1
5 Q×RP	R–B2
6 Q–N8+	R–B1
7 Q–B7	R–B2
8 Q–B8+	R–B1
9 Q×P+	1–0

After 9 ... K–R1 10 Q×P Black loses another pawn. Rook and knight are no match for queen and three pawns in this position.

c) *The Rooks*

The rook is a powerful piece, but it needs space in which to prove its value. The most common method by which a rook plays an active part in the game is by being posted on an open file (i.e. one cleared of pawns). The rook can then penetrate down the board, often to the seventh rank, from which it rakes the enemy position. Like the queen, the rook should be developed behind the minor pieces and pawns.

Two rooks working in conjunction on an open board are very strong. When they are doubled on the seventh rank, with the opposing king confined to the eighth, this is nearly always a winning advantage. In diagram 90 Marshall is prepared to sacrifice a piece to get both his rooks on the seventh rank.

Thomas

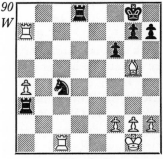

Marshall

White cannot play 1 R×N because of 1 ... R–Q8 mate. Furthermore his bishop is attacked. Marshall's solution to these problems is at first sight surprising, but in fact well thought out.

1 P–R4!

By giving his king an escape square, White frees his rook on QB1 for action—a common stratagem in positions of this kind. Furthermore the advanced KRP is destined to take an active part in the proceedings.

| 1 ... | N–N7 |

Or 1 ... P×B   2 R×N P×P
3 R4–B7 and the doubled rooks
win, much as in the game.

2 R1–B7!

Much stronger than moving the
bishop.

2 ...	**P×B**
3 R×P+	**K–B1**
4 R×RP	**K–N1**

The only practical defence
against mate.

5 RQR7–KN7+	**K–B1**
6 R–QN7!	**K–N1**

Preventing R×N, but ...

7 P–KR5!   1–0

Black has no satisfactory defence against the further advance
of the KRP, e.g. 7 ... R–Q3
8 RR7–QB7 (threatening R–B8
mate) 8 ... R–Q1 9 P–R6 and
Black has no defence against the
mating threat R–KR7 followed
by RN7–N7+ etc.

d) *The Bishops*

The bishop shares with the queen
and rooks the power to go from
one side of the board to the other
in one move, but unlike them, is
restricted to squares of one colour.
This greatly reduces the value of
the bishop. The bishop, therefore,
can (and should) be developed at
an early stage of the game, but
like the more powerful pieces,
requires open spaces in which to
operate to best advantage. In
some cases the bishop is well
developed at KN2 or QN2, the
so-called 'fianchetto'. There is a

variation of the Sicilian Defence
in which Black plays ... B–KN2
and this is called the 'Dragon',
suggestive of a lurking danger.
This move has both offensive and
defensive possibilities (combined
with ... 0–0) and occurs in many
openings such as the Queen's
Indian and King's Indian.

As mentioned previously, two
bishops eliminate the main weakness of one (the colour restriction)
and in an open position they can
generate remarkable power. Diagram 91 illustrates the bishops at
work.

Golombek

91
W

Bronstein

1 P×P	**N–B4**

Or 1 ... P×P   2 Q×Q+ N×Q
3 B×P+ and 4 B×N.

2 P×P	**N×KP**
3 P–Q7!	**N–B4**

If 3 ... Q×Q   4 P–Q8=Q+
and mate follows. And after 3 ...
N×QP 4 Q×Q+ N×Q 5 B–K5+
K–R2 6 B–Q3 wins the knight
(e4).

4 B–K5+   K–R2
5 B–Q3+   1–0

For, if 5 ... K–N1 6 Q–R2+
Q–B2 7 P–Q8=Q mate. The
contrast between the white bishops
raking across the board and the
helpless black knights is most
instructive.

e) *The Knights*

The knight has a peculiar value in
many middle game combinations,
especially when use is made of its
ability to fork and also as a com-
ponent of a direct attacking force
against the king.

Because of the short move and
the ability to jump over other
pieces and pawns, knights come
into their own in blocked positions, when they are normally
more valuable than bishops, or
occasionally rooks. Usually they
should be developed during the
early stages of the game and
should be moved towards the
centre for best effect.

In diagram 92 Black's knights
have a field day.

Black threatens to create a decisive K-side attack by ... R–N2
... P×P and ... R×NP+. So
White tries to get play for his
pieces by sacrificing his centre
pawns.

1 P–Q4   R–N2

Threatening 2 ... P×RP etc.

2 Q–R2   N×KP
3 B–B3   N×QBP
4 P×KP   QP×P

Taimanov

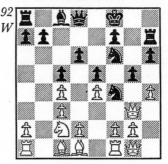

92
W

Portisch

5 B–N2   P–N5!

If Black retreated his knight on
QB6, White might get some
counterplay. But if now 6 B×N
P×B 7 P–N3 N–K7+ 8 K–R1
N×B and wins.

6 B–Q5   NB6–K7+
7 K–R1   P–N6
8 P×P   NK7×P+
9 K–N1   NB5–K7+
10 K–B2   Q–B3+
0–1

Black wins at least a rook.

In order to compare the powers
of bishops and knights, diagrams
91 and 92 should be studied.

f) *The Pawns*

The value of the pawns should not
be underestimated. They are *not*
expendible assets to be sacrificed
at whim; on the contrary they are
extremely valuable. Other things
being equal, the advantage of one
extra pawn will often be sufficient
to win; while two extra pawns
will nearly always win the game.

It was the great French master Philidor who first realised the importance of pawns. 'Pawns are the soul of chess' was how he expressed his belief in their value. Pawns create the backbone of a position, over which the other pieces have to move. In a short chapter like this it is impossible to elucidate all the factors that affect the correct handling of pawns (treatises on the subject are available). The following general principles, to which however there are many exceptions, should be noted:

1: The centre pawns are the most important and one (or both if possible) should be played to the fourth rank at an early stage of the game.

2: Doubled pawns are normally weak. An exception is that in a final race to queen a pawn, the doubled pawns may hold off the approach of the enemy for just one vital move.

3: Isolated pawns should be avoided.

4: Backward pawns, i.e. white pawns Q4, K3 and KB4, black pawns QB5, Q4, KB4—the white pawn at K3 is backward and consequently weak.

5: Passed pawns (the black pawn on QB5 in 4 above) should be advanced as far as possible, always provided that they can be properly supported by the other pieces.

Various examples of the effect of different pawn structures can be seen throughout the text. Diagrams 91 and 92, for instance, illustrate clearly the effect pawns can have. In the open position (diagram 91), with most of the central pawns exchanged, White's bishops dominated the board, but in diagram 92, with no pawns exchanged, the bishops are ineffectual and it is the knights which dominate the play.

Sacrifice

Greek gifts may be proffered at all stages of a game of chess and, if accepted, may lead to the clearance of lines for the use of long-range pieces or to the deflection of enemy units from the path of duty. Examples occur throughout this work. In the middle game we are especially concerned with decisive combinations starting with a sacrifice and ending in checkmate or great material gain.

An attack on the uncastled king by four or five well coordinated pieces will usually succeed, allowing one to be sacrificed in order to break up the K-side position. A common sequence to be guarded against is 1 B×KRP+ K×B 2 N–N5+ K moves 3 Q enters, perhaps at KR5 and 4 Q mates K.

After 0–0, a hostile rook may be in the KR-file and this may be sacrificed on KR8 so as to allow the queen to check on the KR-file. If then the king moves to N1, a second rook may be able to occupy a square on the KR-file and mate by Q–KR8 or R–KR8 could follow. Obviously the other circumstances of the position have to be considered. Such combinations should only be embarked on after full analysis and this must include careful study of the possible counter-attacks, especially when the sequence of checks is interrupted.

Sacrifices, good and bad, abound in the games section (chapter 6). Sound sacrifices can be seen in diagrams 113 and 128, whilst in contrast in diagram 133 Smyslov refutes Keres' ingenious sacrifices by ignoring them! Game no. 5 is particularly interesting: Chigorin sacrifices in vain for an attack, Lasker sacrifices decisively for mate.

4 The Opening

Before discussing the individual openings, it is necessary to consider some general principles governing deployment of forces for attack and defence.

1: Development of the pieces. At the beginning of a game the pieces and pawns are poorly placed: unable to attack the opposing forces or to defend the king. The queen, rooks and bishops are blocked by pawns and cannot move. The square KB2 (f2, or f7 for Black) is defended only by the king and if a supported queen landed thereon she might effect checkmate.

The pieces and pawns are like soldiers in barracks or guns in the arsenal. They have to be brought into action and must be so placed as to work in concert as quickly as possible. Game no. 1 is a drastic illustration of the perils that befall a player who neglects his development.

2: Attack and defence must be coordinated. It is useless to be aggressive if your attack can be repulsed with loss of time, especially if the advance of pieces creates serious weakness at home. An uncoordinated attack came to grief in game no. 5.

3: In general the advance is best made by the lighter forces— pawns, knights, and bishops in that order. Pawns may be likened to infantry, but there is a very important difference in that pawns cannot retreat. It is therefore important to move them only so far as they can be well protected, preferably by another pawn, unless they can be used as battering rams to break up the enemy defences. Other dangers of hasty advance of pawns arise from the effects of exchanges and attack on the supports. Nevertheless an advanced and well defended pawn is a source of strength.

4: At least in the earlier stages the heavier forces, queen and rooks, should be kept near the base line; the queen will usually be moved up one or perhaps two squares so as to allow the rooks to be connected after castling. Later it may be sought to open up a file on which a rook can operate, and still later the rooks may be *doubled* on that file. For example, let us suppose that the KBP has been advanced and 0–0 has been played. Doubling of the rooks can then be carried out by means of the moves R–KB2 and QR–KB1.

5: If possible a strong centre should be established, and the method usually adopted to this end is to occupy the centre with protected pawns. If these are secure, an attack on the king can be made on the left or right centre or on the wings. If the centre is not held, such an attack will rarely succeed. Naturally there are exceptional cases and very many when the attack has a limited objective such as gain of material. The strong centre is like a salient thrust into the enemy position. It restricts his freedom of movement and the forces in the salient are often able to participate in a breakthrough on the right or left. The battle for the centre is probably the most important single factor in modern chess opening play. The centre should never be neglected and every endeavour should be made to place the pieces and pawns so that they have the maximum influence on events in that part of the board.

Perhaps this is a suitable place for the interpolation that *all* rules of policy may be broken if a player discerns a forced continuation leading to mate or great gain of material. In the latter case, however, the possibility of a loss of initiative, and strong recovery by the opposing side must always be considered.

6: We give below a brief outline of some of the principal chess openings. Without attempting detailed analysis, we have chosen a few characteristic variations. They have been selected to give an indication of some of the typical positions that can arise. By contrasting the various methods of development adopted by both sides, the problems arising in different positions can be appreciated. Reference is made to the Games Section (chapter 6) at several points in the text. In these cases, discussion of the opening strategy is further developed in the games concerned.

One of the best opening moves that White can make is 1P–K4. This is a pawn move which frees the king's bishop and queen and stakes a claim to part of the centre. Indeed, if black were to play a bad first move, e.g. 1 . . . P–QR3, White would reply 2P–Q4 with a fine centre. But Black has better alternatives, one of which is 1 . . . P–K4. White's replies can be considered under three alternatives, according to the policy he adopts.

A: White develops quietly.

Giuoco Piano

1 P–K4 P–K4 2 N–KB3 N–QB3 3 B–B4 B–B4 the game could continue:

4 P–Q3 N–B3 5 N–B3 P–Q3 6 B–KN5 P–KR3 7 B×N Q×B 8 N–Q5 Q–Q1 9 P–B3 P–R3 10 P–QN4 B–R2 11 P–QR4 B–K3 12 Q–N3 0–0 13 N–K3 Q–Q2 (*93*).

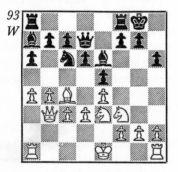

There are a number of aggressive variations based on 4 P–B3, but Black can equalise by . . . N–KB3 and an early . . . P–Q4. Game 5 illustrates play in a gambit variation of this opening.

Four Knights

1 P–K4 P–K4 2 N–KB3 N–QB3 3 N–B3 N–B3.

A typical variation is:

4 B–N5 B–N5 5 0–0 0–0 6 P–Q3 B×N 7 P×B P–Q3 8 B–N5 Q–K2 9 R–K1 N–Q1 10 P–Q4 N–K3 11 B–QB1 R–Q1 (*94*).

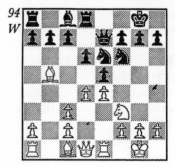

This opening tends to lead to prolonged positional manoeuvring.

Neither of these openings creates serious problems for Black. So let us see what happens when White tries to occupy the centre immediately.

B: White attempts to occupy the centre at an early stage.

Scotch Game

1 P–K4 P–K4 2 N–KB3 N–QB3 3 P–Q4.

Black must capture and the main variation is 3 . . . P×P 4 N×P N–B3 5 N–QB3 B–N5 6 N×N NP×N 7 B–Q3 P–Q4 8 P×P P×P 9 0–0 0–0 10 B–KN5 P–B3 (*95*) and play is about equal. Note how rapidly both sides have developed their pieces.

The Scotch can in fact be recommended for early practice, because it gives White a sound development without too many commitments, which will stand him in good stead during a chess

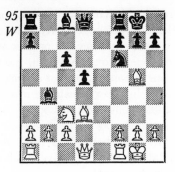

95
W

apprenticeship. An interesting variation is the Scotch Gambit, in which White offers a pawn on move 4 for a lead in development (i.e. material for time), 4 B–QB4 B–B4 5 P–B3 P×P 6 N×P P–Q3 chances are about equal.

King's Gambit*

1 P–K4 P–K4 2 P–KB4

These are the first moves of some of the most brilliant débuts available to the chess player. The idea is that if Black accepts the gambit pawn and tries to hold on to it, White gains compensating attacking chances by N–KB3 B–QB4 P–Q4 0–0 etc. Game 1 gives an excellent illustration of

*A Gambit (from Italian *gambetto*) is an opening in which a pawn (or 2 P's, or sometimes a knight) is offered as a sacrifice in order to gain a positional advantage. We speak of the gambit *accepted* or *declined*. In many cases the sacrifice is temporary in nature and the gambit material can be recovered. A gambit can be declined by a *counter gambit*. E.g. 1 P–K4 P–K4 2 P–KB4 P–Q4 3 KP×P P–K5 (Falkbeer Counter Gambit). This is an enterprising game well worthy of more practical attention.

the complications that can follow.

Unfortunately Black players normally prefer to equalise by counter-sacrifice of the QP at an early stage. This leads to equality but a dull game, e.g. 2 ... P×P 3 N–KB3 P–Q4 4 P×P N–KB3 5 B–N5+ P–B3 (*96*) 6 P×P and Black can equalise by either 6 ... P×P or 6 ... N×P. For this

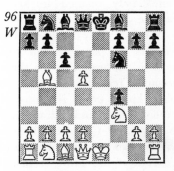

96
W

reason, the King's Gambit is not frequently seen in tournament chess at the present time. Nevertheless its resources are by no means exhausted and club-players will find that a majority of their opponents adopt pet methods of their own which are much weaker than that we have mentioned.

C: White attacks Black's central defences with his pieces.

The Ruy Lopez

1 P–K4 P–K4 2 N–KB3 N–QB3 3 B–N5.

This opening is the strongest we have considered so far and has long been the most frequently adopted continuation after 1 P–K4 P–K4. It is based on a plausible conception of attack and defence and the argument runs as follows. 2 N–KB3 attacked the KP, which was defended by 2 ... N–QB3. Very well—we will attack this support and, after taking it, we can play N×KP. Actually this threat cannot be immediately realised in action because after 3 ... P–QR3 4 B×N QP×B 5 N×P Q–Q5. This recovers the pawn with a good position. Nevertheless, the threat becomes real again after the white king's pawn is protected. In most variations Black will wish to play ... P–Q3, after which he will face an embarrassing pin on his N at QB3. Most of Black's best defences are based on 3 ... P–QR3—Morphy's move which enables Black to play ... P–QN4, driving the bishop away at an opportune moment.

The Ruy Lopez has been intensively analysed for decades. It is undoubtedly not a beginner's début, but once a certain stage of chess skill has been reached, it is one of the most interesting of all chess openings. We give three variations, but they can only be regarded as indications of the very many possibilities.

On account of the extensive analysis of the Lopez, many match players tended to avoid its intricacies and adopted the French, Sicilian, Caro-Kann, or Alekhine defences (q.v.). There are signs of the reverse process at the present time. After all, most of our opponents are not encyclopaedic in their knowledge of the ramifications and the Lopez is at least an *opening* in the true sense. It will get both sides into the middle game and give native talent its chance.

Steinitz Defence Deferred: 3 ... P–QR3 4 B–R4 P–Q3 5 P–Q4 P–QN4 6 B–N3 N×P 7 N×N P×N 8 P–QB3 P×P 9 N×P B–N2 10 Q–K2 P–QB4 11 B–KB4 N–K2 the chances are about equal.

Also: 3 ... P–QR3 4 B–R4 N–B3 5 0–0 P–Q3 6 P–B3 B–Q2 7 P–Q4 B–K2 8 R–K1 0–0=

Chigorin Defence: 3 ... P–QR3 4 B–R4 N–B3 5 0–0 B–K2 6 R–K1 P–QN4 7 B–N3 P–Q3 8 P–B3 0–0 9 P–KR3 N–QR4 10 B–B2 P–B4 11 P–Q4 Q–B2 (97). One of the best known positions in chess theory and the start of innumerable investigations.

The Ruy Lopez is discussed further in Game 2.

The difficulties of playing the Black side of the Ruy Lopez have led players to consider various alternatives on the first move. These defences allow White to occupy the centre. By counter-attacking vigorously, Black can usually secure equality.

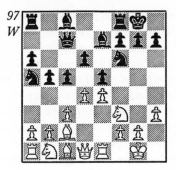

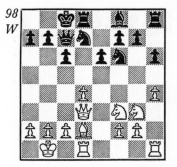

French Defence

1 P–K4 P–K3.

A sound defence. Black secures an adequate hold on the centre by playing ... P–Q4 and ... P–QB4. Its main defect is the bad position of the Black QB which is very difficult to get into adequate play. As this opening is considered in Games 4 and 7, we give no variations here.

Caro-Kann Defence

1 P–K4 P–QB3.

An attempt to avoid the main defect of the French Defence, namely the problem of developing the QB. Primarily a positional opening.

A typical variation is:

2 P–Q4 P–Q4 3 N–QB3 P×P
4 N×P B–B4 5 N–N3 B–N3
6 P–KR4 P–KR3 7 N–B3 N–Q2
8 B–Q3 B×B 9 Q×B Q–B2
10 B–Q2 KN–B3 11 0–0–0 P–K3
12 K–N1 0–0–0 (*98*) with an even position.

Sicilian Defence

1 P–K4 P–QB4.

The fighting defence par excellence. Black makes no attempt to hinder White's moves, but launches immediate counterplay on the black squares. The difficult positions constantly arising in this opening have made it one of the most popular of the day. Among the most critical variations are the following:

The Dragon: 2 N–KB3 P–Q3
3 P–Q4 P×P 4 N×P N–KB3
5 N–QB3 P–KN3 6 B–K3 B–N2
7 P–B3 N–B3 8 Q–Q2 0–0.

The Scheveningen: 2 N–KB3
P–Q3 3 P–Q4 P×P 4 N×P
N–KB3 5 N–QB3 P–K3 (99) and Black develops by ... B–K2 ...
0–0 ... N–QB3 ... B–Q2 and
... Q–B2.

The Najdorf: 2 N–KB3 P–Q3
3 P–Q4 P×P 4 N×P N–KB3
5 N–QB3 P–QR3.

In all cases the complications and alternatives are legion. The Sicilian is also an opening not to

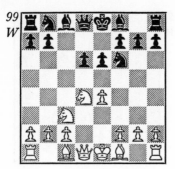

99
W

be recommended to beginners, as Black's defence has to be extremely accurate against the best play. Game 15 gives an excellent example of the troubles that can face Black if he plays incorrectly. Nevertheless, the opening remains very popular because it forces White to play aggressively and well and gives Black good winning chances.

QUEEN'S PAWN OPENINGS

1 P–Q4 is probably the strongest opening move because it a) occupies a strong point in the centre, b) opens lines for the queen and queen's bishop, c) protects KB2 indirectly by restraining the hostile king's bishop. Black's defences are in one of two classes. In the first, he replies 1 ... P–Q4 and, in the second, he allows White to occupy the centre and counter-attacks for equality.

Both players occupy the centre at an early stage. 1 P–Q4 P–Q4.

Something must be done to gain an advantage and in all the openings of this group the struggle is around the centre, both to maintain one's own position and to attack the enemy in this vital region. The key moves are accordingly either P–QB4 or P–K4 because these moves are the only ones that can attack the pawn at Black's Q4 by a pawn. It is instructive to compare the situation with that obtaining in openings based on 1 P–K4 P–K4. The fact that the queen's pawn is protected by the queen means that a piece attack upon it (similar to the piece attack in the Ruy Lopez) is ineffective, so it must be reinforced by a pawn. By far the strongest move for White is 2 P–QB4 which leads to the following variations (inter alia):

2 ... P×P Queen's Gambit Accepted;

2 ... P–K3 Queen's Gambit Declined;

2 ... P–QB3 Slav Defence.

Queen's Gambit Declined

1 P–Q4 P–Q4 2 P–QB4 P–K3 White's second move attacks Black's outpost, which Black in turn defends.

3 N–QB3 N–KB3. White reinforces the attack with a piece and Black in turn defends in a similar manner.

4 B–N5 B–K2.

White pins the defending piece

and Black unpins. The logical basis of the play can be readily perceived. At this stage the various alternatives become complex, but a typical variation is:

5 P–K3 0–0 6 N–B3 QN–Q2
7 R–B1 P–B3 8 B–Q3 P×P
9 B×BP N–Q4 10 B×B Q×B
11 0–0 N×N 12 R×N P–K4=
(*100*).

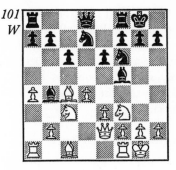

101
W

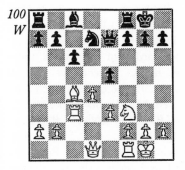

100
W

This opening is discussed further in Games 6 and 9.

Slav Defence

1 P–Q4 P–Q4 2 P–QB4 P–QB3. The main virtue of this defence is the fact that Black can easily develop his queen's bishop—his problem piece in most Q-side openings.

3 N–KB3 N–B3 4 N–B3 P×P
5 P–QR4 B–B4 6 P–K3 P–K3
7 B×P B–QN5 8 0–0 0–0 9 Q–K2
QN–Q2=(*101*).

Game 10 illustrates the strategy of this opening.

Queen's Gambit Accepted

1 P–Q4 P–Q4 2 P–QB4 P×P.

In contrast to the King's Gambit, this is not a true gambit, as White can always recover the pawn. In the following variation Black counter-attacks on the Q-side by:

3 N–KB3 N–KB3 4 P–K3
P–K3 5 B×P P–B4 6 0–0 P–QR3
(*102*) 7 Q–K2 P–QN4 and Black

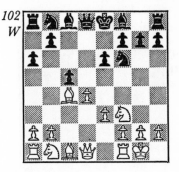

102
W

completes his development by . . . B–N2 . . . QN–Q2 . . . B–K2 etc. The position is approximately equal.

We arrive at the group of openings in which Black allows White to occupy the centre and then counter-attacks. These openings are extremely popular, as they afford excellent chances for both players.

Nimzo-Indian Defence

1 P–Q4 N–KB3 2 P–QB4 P–K3 3 N–QB3 B–N5 Black attempts to prevent White playing P–K4 by the pin on the knight at QB3. White has a number of alternatives. We give two of the most common.

First he can attack the bishop by 4 P–QR3. There might follow: 4 ... B×N+ 5 P×B P–B4 6 P–K3 0–0 7 B–Q3 N–B3 8 N–K2 P–Q3 9 P–K4 N–K1 10 0–0 P–QN3 11 P–B4 P–B4 (*103*) reaching a complex and controversial position with chances for both sides: White's big centre has proved itself alternately weak and strong.

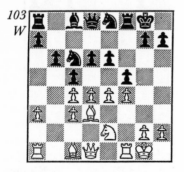

103
W

Secondly, White supports his centre:

4 P–K3 0–0 5 B–Q3 P–Q4 6 N–B3 P–B4 7 0–0 N–B3 8 P–QR3 B×N 9 P×B QP×P 10 B×BP Q–B2.

Another variant is analysed in Game 8.

Game no. 11 considers the related Queen's Indian Defence.

King's Indian Defence

1 P–Q4 N–KB3 2 P–QB4 P–KN3 3 N–QB3 B–N2.

It is very difficult to give an exact order of moves, as there are many alternatives at all stages, but the defence is characterised by the Black moves ... N–KB3 ... P–KN3 ... B–N2 ... P–Q3 and ... 0–0. White can develop P–Q4 P–QB4 P–K4 P–KB4 and occupy the centre. But Black is not neglecting the centre. At the right time he will play ... P–K4, or perhaps even ... P–QB4 and will endeavour to prove that White's strong looking centre can be destroyed (diagram 88 shows an example). It is probably better for White to delay P–KB4, or to substitute P–KB3 and to complete development of his pieces as quickly as possible, before advancing in the centre.

Play can continue:

4 P–K4 P–Q3 5 N–B3 0–0 6 B–K2 P–K4 7 0–0 (*104*) QN–Q2 8 P–Q5 N–B4 9 Q–B2 P–QR4 or 4 P–K4 P–Q3 5 P–B3 0–0 6 B–K3 P–K4 7 P–Q5

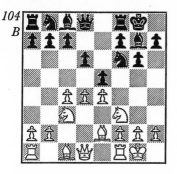

104
B

P–B3   8 Q–Q2 P×P   9 BP×P
P–QR3.

A popular variation of the King's Indian is discussed in Games 12 and 13, which show wins for White and for Black. Game no. 14 considers a pawn formation very common in this opening.

English, Reti and Similar Openings

It did not take chess players long to realise that an effective defence for Black might make a powerful opening for White. Indeed this method of opening can be particularly effective if Black is too ambitious, as a good defence, allied with White's extra move, can lead to a clear advantage. If Black contents himself with a more modest development, he should equalise without difficulty.

English Opening

1 P–QB4. A Sicilian in reverse and Black gets a difficult game if he copies White's normal strategy, e.g.

1 P–QB4 P–K4   2 N–QB3 N–KB3 3 P–KN3 P–Q4 4 P×P N×P 5 B–N2 N–N3 6 N–B3 N–B3 7 P–QR3 B–K3 8 P–Q3 P–B3 9 P–QN4 White has the advantage.

Black does better by striking an independent path.

1 P–QB4 P–K4   2 N–QB3 N–QB3 3 P–KN3 P–KN3   4 B–N2 B–N2 5 P–Q3 KN–K2 6 N–B3 P–Q3 7 0–0 0–0 with about equal chances. White's pressure on the Q-side is offset by Black's chances of an attack on the K-side.

Reti Opening

1 N–KB3 P–Q4 2 P–B4.

The difficulties that face Black if he makes too many pawn moves are illustrated by the following variation:

2 ... P–Q5 3 P–KN3 P–QB4 4 B–N2 N–QB3   5 0–0 P–K4 6 P–Q3 B–K2   7 P–QN4 P×P 8 P–QR3 P×P   9 Q–R4 and White's pawn sacrifice gives him an excellent game with strong pressure on the centre and Q-side. Game no. 16 is a splendid example of White's possibilities.

A more satisfactory defensive formation is known as the London System. Note how White attempts to control the centre by his fianchettoed bishops, while Black contents himself with a modest pawn centre which is much harder to attack than in the variation given above.

1 N–KB3 P–Q4 2 P–QB4 P–QB3 3 P–QN3 N–B3 4 P–KN3 B–B4 5 B–KN2 P–K3 6 B–N2 QN–Q2 7 0–0 B–Q3 8 P–Q3 0–0 (*105*) with an equal position.

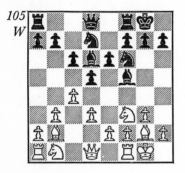

105
W

A comparison of the positions in diagrams 93–105 shows the wide variety of possibilities that exist after only a small number of moves.

This short survey is no more than a brief introduction to a complex and fascinating subject. Many openings, some of considerable importance, have necessarily been omitted, but by studying the variations given, in conjunction with the selected games in chapter 6, it is hoped that it will be found possible to explore opening play in a preliminary manner adequate for early practical needs.

Suggestions for further reading are given in the bibliography in chapter 7.

5 The Endgame

Nothing distinguishes the master from the amateur more than his ability to play the endgame well. Indeed at the highest levels of chess it is essential to be a very strong endgame player. All the world champions have been experts in this respect and many of them have been outstanding, e.g. Steinitz, Lasker, Capablanca, Botvinnik, Smyslov and Fischer. The great advantage conferred by such proficiency is that it enables its possessor to forecast accurately the result of exchanges or other tactics which can transform the middle game into an endgame. At such junctures a somewhat eccentric member of a Chess Club in the Antipodes was in the habit of drawing on a pair of white cotton gloves, reminiscent of Wagner's gesture when he conducted Mendelssohn's music. The endgame use of this symbol implied: my friends, we have reached the mathematical phase.

More often than not the amateur neglects the endgame and hence plays it badly. If the reason for this is that the endgame is thought to be uninteresting and a matter of dull technique, then nothing could be further from the truth, as the endgame is often characterised by complex and subtle play. Furthermore, its study confers the very practical advantage of pointing the way to the efficient conversion of an advantage into a win and to putting up the best resistance when in difficulties. Nothing could be more frustrating than spoiling a well played game, having perhaps won a pawn, and yet only drawing because of floundering in the endgame.

It is easy to spend too much time on study of the opening, to the detriment of acquirement of knowledge of the endgame. It is not sufficiently well recognised that the study of the endgame strengthens a player's middle game and even his opening skill. An example in the opening is the purposeful securing of a majority of pawns on the side on which the king is not castled.

The topic is vast and the standard text book on the subject has over 550 closely printed pages. Yet even this major work can only be regarded as an introduction to the subject! Nevertheless, we can give a few of the general rules of endgame play and illustrate these with examples from master play.

1: Endgame play is usually dominated by the desire to effect pawn promotion. Apart from problem positions, a player must be at least a rook ahead to force mate. Therefore, unless he has this material advantage in hand, a player must, in order to force mate, queen one of his pawns. The additional queen tips the balance of power decisively in his favour. In fact the defender will normally be forced to sacrifice one of his pieces to prevent the pawn queening. The additional piece can then be used to capture more pawns; these in turn can be queened. In this way, sufficient superiority of force will be created to force mate. It follows that if a player has a material advantage, then he must use it to capture pawns.

2: The player who is a pawn(s) ahead should endeavour to exchange pieces, but not pawns. The defender should, of course, try to do the reverse. This rule derives logically from 1 above.

3: If a player has two or more

pawns plus, the win can normally be achieved by the straightforward advance of the pawns to queen. But if the advantage is only one pawn, then the problem can be much more difficult, as the direct advance will not usually succeed *per se*. A winning technique which is frequently used employs one of the pawns as a decoy. While the defending pieces capture or blockade the pawn, the other pieces (very often the king) penetrate the enemy position and capture further pawns. Note that lone pawns are quite defenceless against attack unless they can quickly move out of range.

4: follows logically from 3 above; the defending party has excellent drawing chances if all the pawns are on the same side of the board—because the superior party will find it almost impossible to create a decoy as in 3 above.

5: The king is a strong piece: use it! A good king's position can often be a decisive factor.

Further principles will become apparent from the examples below.

In our first endgame (*106*), Black has a number of advantages:
a) He has an extra pawn which is an outside passed pawn.
b) His king is one square nearer the centre.
c) The bishop is probably superior to the knight in this particular

Nimzowitsch

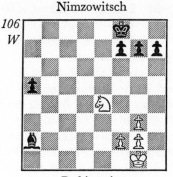

Rubinstein

open position. This is not a reliable generalisation.

In the circumstances, Black can win quickly:

1 N–B3

White is unable to centralise his king immediately, e.g. 1 K–B1 B–B5+ 2 K–K1 B–Q4 forcing the exchange of pieces or winning another pawn. After 3 P–B3 B×N 4 P×B K–K2 5 K–K2 K–K3 6 K–K3 K–K4 Black wins easily by advancing his QRP. The white king has to go in pursuit and while he is away, the black king captures all White's pawns. This is the decoy technique in its simplest and most effective form (Rule 3). Note how the exchange of pieces facilitates Black's win (Rule 2). Both sides now centralise their kings (Rule 5).

1 ...	B–B5
2 P–B4	K–K2
3 K–B2	K–Q3
4 K–K3	K–B4

The white king has arrived too late to prevent the black king supporting his pawn. But if the white king had been able to reach Q4 the win would have been much harder. This is discussed later. Now Black wins with great ease.

5 P–N4	K–N5
6 K–Q4	B–N6
7 P–N5	P–R5
8 N–N1	B–K3
9 P–N3	K–N6
10 N–B3	P–R6
11 K–Q3	P–N3
12 K–Q4	K–B7
0–1	

Now let us see what happens if we give White an extra move so that he could play 4K–Q4 above. Play might continue:

4 K–Q4 B–N6 5 P–N4 P–R5 6 N–N5+ K–K3 7 P–N3 B–Q8 8 P–N5 K–B4 9 K–K3 K–N5 10 K–B2.

White has placed all his pawns on black squares so that they cannot be attacked by the bishop. If Black plays 10 ... K–B4 11K–K3 keeps the black king out. But Black can manoeuvre with his bishop against the knight, which is handicapped by the necessity to watch the QRP.

10 ... B–B7! 11 N–R3 B–Q6!

White is in 'Zugzwang'. This word is used when a player has arranged his pieces in the most favourable manner, but the compulsion of the move forces him to alter the position to his disadvantage. The present position is a

good example. White would be
quite happy not to move, but he
must and he loses. If the knight
moves it is captured; if 12 K–N2
K–B4 13 K–B2 K–K5 and the
black king has penetrated the
position and wins as in the game;
lastly if 12 K–K3 K×P/N6! 13
K×B K×P followed by ... K×P
and White can stop the passed
pawns on only one side of the
board. Nevertheless, White has
put up a much better resistance
than in the game and Black had
to play accurately to win—a good
illustration of the value of a
centralised king.

If Black's extra pawn at QR4
was placed at K3 say, the
position is drawn, as Black cannot
create an outside passed pawn
(Rule 4).

Our next example (*107*), is a
tribute to the power of an outside
passed pawn.

Tartakower

Schlechter

Black can draw easily by cen-
tralising his king. Thus: 1 ...

K–B1 2 K–Q3 K–K2 3 K–B4
K–Q2 4 K–B5 K–B2 5 P–QR4
P–N3+ (essential otherwise 6 P–
QR5 and Black loses, as White
can invade QN6) 6 K–B4 K–B3
and White cannot penetrate the
position—drawn. But instead,
Black made an instructive error,
which loses as it enables White to
obtain an outside passed KRP.

1 ...	**P–KN4?**
2 P×P	**P×P**
3 K–B3	**K–N3**
4 K–N4	**P–B4+**

If Black does nothing, White
proceeds as in the game—P–KN3
followed by P–KR4.

5 P×Pep	**K×P**
6 P–KN3	**P–R4**
7 P–QR4	

To prevent Black blocking
White's Q-side pawns. White now
advances his KRP until Black is
forced to capture it. While the
black king is performing this task,
his rival sets off for the Q-side and
the unprotected black pawns.

7 ...	**P–K4**
8 P–R4!	**P×P**
9 P×P	**K–N3**
10 P–N3	**P–N3**
11 P–R5+	**K–B3**
12 P–R6	**K–N3**
13 P–R7	**K×P**
14 K–B5	**1–0**

Black cannot prevent White
from capturing all his pawns.

As an example of how master
players integrate the endgame
into their overall strategy the

reader should consider diagram 127, Game no. 8. Alekhine executes a profound combination with the basic aim of reaching an easily won king and pawn ending.

Our next example is very typical of positions that often arise.

van Doesburgh

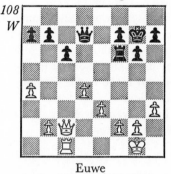

Euwe

White has won a pawn, but there are no immediate prospects of creating a passed pawn. How then should White proceed? Let us see how a world champion goes about it.

1 Q–QB5!

A good move, facing Black with a difficult choice. If 1 ... P–QR3 then 2 Q–K5 and the pin immobilises the king and rook. White would follow with R–B3–QN3 tying Black up completely. If 1 ... P–QN3 2 Q–K5 and by playing P–QN4–QN5 White creates a passed QP. So, Black offers the exchange of queens. Naturally this suits White, who is exchanging pieces, not pawns (Rule 2).

1 ...	Q–B4
2 Q×Q	R×Q
3 K–B1	K–B1
4 R–B5	

A typical move. Black cannot exchange, as the king and pawn ending is easily won for White. Therefore he has to retreat, but White will put his well placed rook to work, as we shall see. This is an often recurring dilemma for the defender. He must avoid exchanges, but if he does so, his own pieces are continually driven back to passive positions. Note that White could not play 3 R–B5 because 3 ... R×R! 4 P×R K–B3 5 P–B4 K–B4 6 K–B2 K–K5 7 K–K2 K–Q4 8 P–QN4 K–B5 and *Black* wins!

4 ...	R–B3
5 R–QR5!	

An important move, weakening Black's Q-side pawns. There is now a potential point of entry for the white king at QN6.

5 ...	P–QR3
6 R–K5	

Cutting the black king off from the centre.

6 ...	R–Q3
7 P–R5!	

Fixing the weakness

7 ...	P–B3

Black decides that he must use his king to defend the Q-side, so he drives away the rook, but in doing so he weakens his K-side pawns.

8 R–QB5	K–K2

9 P–KN4	P–R3
10 K–K2	R–K3
11 P–B4	R–Q3
12 P–R4	K–B2
13 P–R5	

During the last few moves, White has advanced his pawn majority on the K-side. However Black plays now, he will be forced to make further concessions. If now 13 ... P–KN4 14 P×P BP×P (14 ... RP×P gives White a passed KRP) 15 R–B5+, cutting off the king from one side of the board, followed by K–Q3 and P–K4–K5 with a won position. So he exchanges, but his K-side pawns are weakened thereby.

13 ...	P×P
14 R×RP	K–N3
15 K–Q3	R–Q2
16 P–K4	K–N2
17 P–N5!	

Dissolving the K-side pawns and creating—at last—a passed pawn.

17 ...	BP×P
18 P×P	K–N3
19 R×P+	K×P
20 R–R2	

Threatening R–KB2, cutting off the black king.

20 ...	K–B3
21 P–K5+	K–K3
22 R–R6+	K–Q4
23 P–N4!	R–Q1

Black is move-bound. White now settles the matter with a few sharp strokes.

| 24 R–R7 | R–QN1 |
| 25 R–K7! | P–N3 |

Zugswang again.

| 26 R–Q7+ | K–K3 |
| 27 R–Q6+ | 1–0 |

He loses another pawn, with a hopeless position. An impressive example of the technique of a world champion.

The next two endings contrast the powers of bishop against knight and illustrate the effect that small alterations in the position can make to the fortunes of either side.

In diagram 56 Black has the following advantages:

Lasker

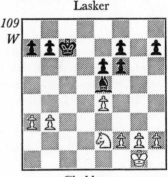

Chekhover

In diagram 109 Black has the following advantages:

a) Better king position.

b) The bishop is superior to the knight, as there are pawns on both sides of the board.

c) The white Q-side pawns are weak and susceptible to attack by the black king and bishop.

1 K–B1

White centralises his king. If he tries 1 P–QR4 K–N3 2 P–QN4 B–Q3 3 P–N5 K–R4 4 N–B3 B–K4 and the pawns fall.

1 . . .   P–QN4

Endgame play demands considerable accuracy and Dr. Lasker, one of the finest endgame players in the history of chess, plays with great precision. An attempt to win as in the previous game only draws: 1 . . . B–N7 2 P–QR4 K–N3 3 K–K1 K–R4 4 K–Q2 K–N5 5 K–B2, protecting the pawns with the king.

2 K–K1	B–N7
3 P–QR4	P×P
4 P×P	K–B3

Once again Lasker avoids a false trail: 4 . . . K–N3 5 K–Q2 K–R4 6 K–B2 B–K4 7 P–B4 B–Q3 8 K–N3 and White can hold the ending.

5 K–Q2	K–B4
6 N–B3	

White observes that he cannot play 6 K–B2 B–Q5 (attacking the KBP) 7 P–B3 as 7 .. K–B5! wins because after either 8 N×B K×N 9 K–N3 P–QR4 or 8 N–B1 B–K4 9 P–R3 K–N5, the vital QRP falls. So White sends his knight off on an excursion hoping to attack Black's pawns.

6 . . .	K–N5
7 N–N5	P–QR4
8 N–Q6	K×P
9 K–B2	

Another unfortunate necessity.

White has no time for 9 N×P e.g 9 . . . K–N6 10 N–Q8 P–R5 11 N×P P–R6 12 N–B5+ K–B5 and White must either lose his knight or allow the pawn to queen.

9 . . .	B–K4
10 N×P	B×P

So Black remains a pawn up. The rest is easy.

11 N–Q8	P–K4
12 N–B6	B–N8
13 P–B3	B–B4
14 N–N8	K–N4
15 P–N4	B–K2
16 P–N5	

Forced, Black threatened to capture the wandering knight.

16 . . .	P×P
17 N–Q7	B–Q3
18 N–B6	K–B5
0–1	

After 19 N×P B–K2 traps the knight and his helplessness is manifest.

Woliston

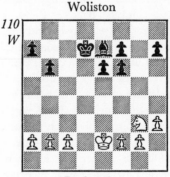

110
W

Reshevsky

White's position in diagram 110 is clearly better than in diagram 109. For one thing, his king is centralised. Furthermore, his Q-side pawns are strong and he will eventually be able to obtain a passed pawn, while his opponent's majority is devalued by the doubled KBP. Nevertheless, Black is far from lost—the bishop is potentially superior to the knight and he only loses because he makes several mistakes.

Reshevsky's plan is to block the position and so reduce the effectiveness of the bishop, before creating a passed pawn on the Q-side. Play proceeded:

1 K–Q3	K–B3
2 N–K2	B–B4
3 P–KB4	P–N4?

As a general principle, it is correct strategy to place pawns on the squares of the opposite colour to his bishop. In this way the bishop's mobility is preserved. But Black chooses the wrong pawn. He should undoubtedly have played 3 ... P–B4 to restrain White's K-side advance and to free the diagonal a1–h8 for his bishop. After this it would be very difficult (if possible at all) for White to win. But the text is also premature in itself, as it assists White in his task of creating a passed pawn on the Q-side. It would be better to leave his Q-side pawns alone at this stage until it is clear how White intends to proceed.

| 4 P–KN4 | P–QR3 |
| 5 K–K4 | |

Now ... P–B4 is permanently prevented and the white king is well posted in the centre of the board.

5 ...	B–B1
6 N–Q4+	K–Q3
7 N–N3	B–K2
8 N–Q2	B–B1
9 P–B4	K–B4
10 P×P	P×P?

After the pawn exchange White is a step nearer his passed pawn, but Black should have either exchanged pawns himself or played 10 ... K×P as the pawn on QN4 is more susceptible to attack than would be a pawn on QR3. Now he is probably lost.

11 N–N3+	K–Q3
12 N–Q4	K–B4
13 P–B5!	

This thrust reveals how bad Black's game has become. If 13 ... P×P+ 14 N×BP and White wins easily due to Black's weak pawns (particularly on KB2), e.g. 14 ... K–B3 15 P–R3 K–B4 16 P–N3 K–B3 17 P–N4 and if the bishop moves 18 N–R6 and if 17 ... K–Q2 18 K–Q5 and wins.

| 13 ... | P–K4 |

But now Black has a 'bad' bishop, i.e. one restricted by its own pawns and as a result he is weak on the white squares. White's next move threatens P–N5, which Black prevents—but another black pawn goes on to a black square.

14 N–B3	P–R3
15 P–KR4	B–K2
16 P–R5	

White has prepared a breakthrough, of which this move is the first step.

| 16 ... | B–Q3 |
| 17 P–R3 | |

The game continuation was 17 ... P–N5 18 P–R4 P–N6 19 N–Q2 K–N5 20 P–R5 K×P 21 N–B4+ 1–0.

Reshevsky gives the following analysis, which shows how his plan would have worked out.

17 ...	K–B5
18 N–Q2+	K–B4
19 P–N4+	K–B3
20 N–B3	B–B1
21 P–N5!	RP×P
22 N–R2	B–N2
23 N–N4	K–Q3
24 P–R6	B–R1
25 P–R7	B–N2
26 N–R6	K–K2
27 K–Q5	K–K1
28 K–B6	P–K5

29 N–N4 and wins.

An ending which emphasises how much scope there can be in the endgame for worthwhile strategy and the very real prospects that exist of outplaying an opponent in this stage of the game. The pitiful rôle played by the bishop in this game contrasts with the part it played in the Lasker ending.

Our final position (*111*) is an illustration of the superiority of an aggressively placed piece over a passive (defending) one. In no endgame is this more marked than rook and pawn endgames.

Rubinstein

Schlechter

The position appears to be more or less equal, but Rubinstein follows a four-part plan that will lead to complete success:

a) The white rook will be pinned down to the defence of his pawns on the K-side.

b) The black king will be centralised.

c) Black's pawn majority will be advanced in order to obtain a passed pawn on the K-side.

d) This gives White two alternatives:

d1) If his king comes over to the K-side, Black will capture material.

d2) If he goes over to the Q-side, Black will create a passed pawn and force it through to queen.

| 1 ... | R–K3 |

2 R–K1

Or 2 R–N3 R–KB3 3 R–N2 R–B6 4 R–K2 as in the game.

| 2 ... | **R–KB3** |
| **3 R–K2** | |

He must prevent 3 ... R–B7.

| 3 ... | **K–K3** |

Stage 1 is already complete, so Black proceeds to stage 2, the centralisation of his king.

| **4 K–B2** | **K–K4** |
| **5 P–B4** | |

White realises what is in store for him and opts for d2 above, utilising his Q-side majority. That d1 would have been hopeless can be easily shown, e.g. 5 K–Q2 K–K5 6 K–K1 R–B6 7 K–Q2 P–KN4 8 R–N2 P–N5 9 R–K2 P–R5 10 R–N2 P–B4 11 R–K2 P–N6 12 P×P P×P 13 R–K1 R–B7+ 14 R–K2 P–N7! and wins.

| 5 ... | **K–K5** |

Part 2 complete; part 3 now commences.

6 P–N4	**P–KN4**
7 K–B3	**P–N5**
8 P–B5	**P–R5**
9 R–KN2	**R–N3**

The last two moves exemplify an important principle of rook and pawn endings, first enunciated by Tarrasch namely: 'The rook's proper place is behind the passed pawn, whether it be his own or an enemy one.' The truth of this maxim is clearly illustrated in the following play:

10 K–B4	**P–N6**
11 RP×P	**RP×P**
12 K–N5	**P×P**
13 P×P	**K–B6**
14 R–N1	**P–R3+!**
0–1	

Making use of his active rook, Rubinstein concludes with an elegant move forcing back the white king. After 15 K–B4 P–N7 16 K–Q5 K–B7 17 R×P+ R×R 18 P–B6 K×P wins easily. A beautiful ending, by one of the best rook and pawn endgame players who ever lived.

It is hoped that the various examples will not only have illustrated and emphasised the necessity to play the endgame well, but will also have provided a glimpse of the kaleidoscopic fascination of this part of the game.

6 Selected Games

The purpose of this chapter is twofold. First it is an attempt to bring together all that has gone before. The reader will see how the principles expounded on earlier pages are utilised in the course of an actual game by introducing some of the greatest masters. Second, the games are a short history of chess, introducing some of the finest players from the middle of the nineteenth century to the present day. Chess theory has evolved (and is evolving) and a brief outline is given of some of the major changes. Maximum benefit will be obtained if the games are played through in their historical sequence. The sixteen games are amongst the finest played and illustrate the drama, excitement and beauty of top class chess. In each case the name of the White player appears first.

Adolf Anderssen 1818–1879

We have not the space to examine the early development of chess and such figures as Giachino (El)

Greco 1600–1634, Francois André (Danican) Philidor 1726–1795 (the first player to appreciate the value of pawns) and Louis Charles de la Bourdonnais and Alexander Macdonnell who played a notable series of matches (won by the first named) the first games on which modern critical judgement can reasonably be directed and Howard Staunton, Anderssen's predecessor.

Modern chess history is normally deemed to have begun with the first international chess tournament held in London in 1851, which was decisively won by the German professor of mathematics, Anderssen, who from then on was generally regarded as the world's strongest player. The secret of Anderssen's success was his extraordinary powers of combination. The chess style of the time was based entirely on attack and counter-attack with gambits and sacrifices the order of the day. In such conditions Anderssen's combinative genius had endless opportunities for expression and he created a large number of brilliant

games which have survived to the
present day. The following game
is very typical of the style of play
prevalent at the time and of
Anderssen's great gifts.

1) *Rosanes–Anderssen*
   Breslau 1863
   King's gambit
1 P–K4	P–K4
2 P–KB4	P×P
3 N–KB3	

The King's Knight Gambit.
Other continuations are the
Bishop's Gambit 3 B–B4 and the
Breyer Gambit 3 Q–B3.

3 . . .   P–KN4

It is this move that makes
White's opening a true gambit;
White cannot regain his pawn by
force, but he can obtain a compensating attack. Whether it is
sufficient remains a matter of
debate. Black can of course
equalise easily by not holding
on to the KBP, as shown in the
analysis on openings.

4 P–KR4	P–N5
5 N–K5	

The Kieseritzky Gambit. The
alternative is the Allgaier Gambit
(5 N–N5) which also gives White
a fierce attack even though he has
to sacrifice the knight after 5 . . .
P–KR3 6 N×BP.

5 . . .   N–KB3

A good alternative is fian-
chettoing the bishop on KN2.

6 B–B4

The obvious attacking move,
but 6 P–Q4 may be better.
Rubinstein considered that 6
B–B4 was incorrect as Black can
free his game by his next move.
He suggested 6 P–Q4 in order to
immediately attack Black's advanced K-side pawns. One variation is 6 . . . P–Q3 7 N–Q3 N×P
8 B×P Q–K2 9 Q–K2 B–N2
10 P–B3 P–KR4? 11 N–Q2 with
the better game.

6 . . .   P–Q4

Essential. Black returns a pawn
to free his game and to block
White's attack.

7 P×P	B–Q3
8 P–Q4	N–R4
9 B–N5+?	

Definitely wrong. White pur-
sues material gain at the expense
of his development and suffers the
inevitable consequences. The best
move is 9 N–QB3 with many
complications, or 9 0–0 Q×P 10
Q–K1 Q×Q 11 R×Q 0–0 12
B–Q3 with equality.

9 . . .	P–QB3
10 P×P	P×P! (*112*)

Very fine judgement—Black is
prepared to sacrifice a whole
rook. Even Morphy, in 1858,
played against Harrwitz 10 . . .
0–0 11 P×P B×P 12 Q×P+
N–N2 13 B×P when White has
much the better game.

11 N×QBP	N×N
12 B×N+	K–B1!

A very fine move. 12 . . . B–Q2
13 B×B+ Q×B 14 0–0 with a

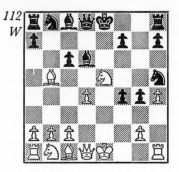

112
W

playable game for White. Sacrificing a rook gives Black an enormous attack as White cannot castle.

13 B×R	N–N6
14 R–R2	

In keeping with the times, White now holds on to his material advantage. A more prudent defence was 14 K–B2 but, according to an analysis by Anderssen, Black would have won by 14 ... N×R+ 15 Q×N B–KB4 16 B–Q5 K–N2 17 N–B3 R–K1 18 B–B6 P–N6+ 19 K–B1 B×P 20 B×R Q×B 21 B–Q2 B–Q6+ 22 K–N1 Q–K4 23 Q–R3 (23 P×Q B–QB4+ mates) 23 ... Q×P+ 24 K–R1 P–B6 25 P×P (25 R–KN1 Q×R+ 26 K×Q P–B7+ and 27 ... P–B8=Q mate) 25 ... B–KB4 and wins—26 Q×B Q×P+ and mates.

14 ...	B–KB4
15 B–Q5	K–N2!
16 N–B3	R–K1+

The point of his 15th move.

17 K–B2	Q–N3

Threatening 18 ... B–K4. It is noticeable how strong Black's pawns on KB5 and KN5 have become—White is being punished for neglecting them in the early stage of the game.

18 N–R4	Q–R3
19 N–B3	B–K4!
20 P–R4 (*113*)	

Hopeless, but Black's pieces are obviously too powerful. If 20 P×B Q–QN3+ 21 K–K1 R×P+ and wins. Anderssen now *announced mate in four moves.*

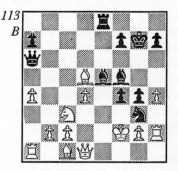

113
B

20 ...	Q–B8+!
21 Q×Q	B×QP+
22 B–K3	R×B!
23 K–N1	R–K8mate

A game dominated by tactics, and in Anderssen's hands these gave rise to brilliant play. But positional considerations have been almost entirely neglected. It was Morphy who brought these factors to the forefront and in so doing dominated the chess world. Once again the player who neglected his development lost the game.

Paul Morphy 1837–1884

The chess career of Morphy was a comet that dazzled the chess world with its brilliance, but a comet that never returned. Born in New Orleans, Morphy was already a master player in his early teens. After decisively winning the American chess congress of 1858, Morphy came to Europe the same year and swept all before him culminating in a crushing victory over Anderssen 7:2 with 2 draws. Morphy returned to America in May 1859. Alas, the story now saddens. Afflicted by a neurosis, Morphy gave up serious chess. For some years he played only with a few close personal friends. Finally, Morphy gave up chess altogether and came to hate the game.

Morphy was a very fine combinative player and the large number of brilliancies he has left us has led to the popular belief that Morphy dominated the chess world by his tactical skill. But Anderssen was a combinative genius. It was therefore not in this area that Morphy's superiority lay. Morphy was the world's first accomplished position player. His understanding of the necessity of development, his appreciation of the centre and open lines, his general understanding of positional factors, was far ahead of his contemporaries. While Anderssen would try to attain positions suitable for his combinative powers, Morphy adopted combination only when the position warranted it.

Morphy's chess exerts a spell even to this day, for his style at its best had a clarity and elegance that has lived over the years. The game against the Duke of Brunswick ... illustrates the effortless way he dealt with weak players. Morphy has been aptly described as 'The pride and sorrow of chess'.

2) *Morphy–Löwenthal*
   Matchgame 14, London 1858
   Ruy Lopez

1 P–K4	P–K4
2 N–KB3	N–QB3
3 B–N5	P–QR3
4 B–R4	N–B3
5 P–Q4	

An obvious attempt to gain control of the centre; however, it is premature as Black can equalise if he plays accurately, but Morphy always played directly for control of the centre.

5 ...	P×P
6 P–K5	N–K5
7 0–0	N–B4
8 B×N	QP×B
9 N×P	N–K3

Not a mistake; but Black can equalise more easily by 9 ... B–K2 e.g. 10 N–QB3 0–0 11 B–K3 R–K1 12 R–K1 B–B1 13 P–B4 P–B3; Alekhine—Keres, Kemeri 1937.

| 10 N×N | B×N |

11 Q–K2 B–QB4?

A mistake, but the right move is not obvious. Black has two major problems:

a) a position must be found for his queen when White plays R–Q1:

b) White has an active majority of pawns on the K-side and the advance P–KB4–KB5 would be extremely awkward.

Furthermore, Black must endeavour to avoid the exchange of one of his bishops as these are his main compensation for his doubled pawns. 11 ... B–K2 is unsatisfactory, after 12 N–B3 0–0 13 B–K3 followed by 14 QR–Q1 embarrasses the queen. Löwenthal's move seems reasonable as the queen can go to K2 and the bishop on QB4 pins the KBP. But the move is wrong as Morphy demonstrates. The correct move was 11 ... Q–R5 threatening B–QB5, if then 12 N–Q2 0–0–0 with chances for both sides, or if 12 R–K1 B–K2 and with the rook on K1 Black does not face the advance P–KB4–B5.

12 N–B3 Q–K2
13 N–K4 P–R3

Otherwise 14 B–N5 but Morphy gains time by his next move.

14 B–K3 B×B
15 Q×B B–B4

Black's aim is to exchange off the knight and hold back the KBP. But Black still has not been able to castle and Morphy takes elegant advantage of this.

16 N–N3! B×P
17 P–B4 P–KN3 (*114*)

Preventing 18 P–B5 which cuts off the bishop. Or if 17 ... Q–N5 18 R–B2 Q×NP 19 R–QB1 wins the bishop.

18 P–K6!

Morphy's genius in open positions asserts itself. He threatens 19 Q–QB3, forking the KR and the bishop and if 18 ... 0–0–0 19 Q–R7 with a decisive attack, Löwenthal finds the only practical defence.

18 ... B–B4
19 N×B P×N
20 P×P+ K×P

Black has gained a pawn, but his K-side pawns are weak, and Morphy has judged—correctly—that he can systematically build up pressure on Black's position. It was in evaluations of this nature that Morphy was so far in advance of his contemporaries.

21 Q–KR3 Q–B3
22 QR–K1 QR–K1
23 R–K5

Occupying a strong point in the centre of the board, as Black cannot exchange 23 ... R×R 24 P×R Q×P 25 R×P+.

23 ...	K–N3
24 R1–K1	R×R
25 R×R	R–Q1
26 Q–KN3+	K–R2
27 P–KR3	R–Q2
28 Q–K3	P–N3
29 K–R2	P–B4
30 Q–K2	Q–N3
31 R–K6	Q–N2
32 Q–R5	R–Q4

33 P–QN3! (*115*)

Morphy has made steady progress during the last few moves. If the reader examines Black's various alternatives, he will see that Black had no satisfactory way of preventing the infiltration of the white pieces. Now he is in Zugzwang and he cannot move his pieces without loss, e.g. 33 ... Q–B1   34 Q–N6+ K–R1   35 R–K8. So Black must move his pawns.

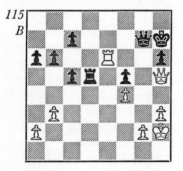

| 33 ... | P–N4 |

Or 33 ... P–QR4 34 P–QR4 and again Black is stuck.

34 R×QRP	R–Q3
35 Q×BP+	Q–N3
36 Q×Q+	K×Q

The endgame is easily won, but nevertheless Morphy handles it perfectly. It serves as a reminder that Morphy was also a finer endgame player than any of his rivals.

37 R–R5	R–N3
38 P–KN4	P–B3
39 K–N3	P–R4
40 R–R7	P×P
41 P×P	K–B3
42 P–B5	K–K4
43 R–K7+	K–Q3
44 P–B6	R–N1
45 P–N5	R–KB1
46 K–B4	P–B5
47 P×P	P×P
48 K–B5	P–B6
49 R–K3	1–0

The superior quality of Morphy's strategy is clearly shown by this game.

Wilhelm Steinitz 1836–1900

Once it became obvious that Morphy had retired from practical play, Anderssen was again regarded as the world's strongest player. He was finally defeated in 1866 by the Viennese master, Steinitz, then living in London. It became apparent by the mid-eighties that Steinitz and the gifted Zukertort were the leading masters of the day. They met in a match played in the United States in 1886, which was the first official match for the world championship, and Steinitz won 10:5 with 5 draws. Steinitz successfully defended his title in matches against Chigorin (twice) and Gunsberg, finally losing it to Dr. Emmanuel Lasker in 1894.

Steinitz was the profoundest and deepest chess thinker in chess history and he created the basis on which modern chess is played. It was Steinitz who first realised the value of defence, who first enunciated the effect of the systematic accumulation of advantages, who first understood the nature of closed positions and who developed a true understanding of the centre. Morphy certainly appreciated some of these factors, perhaps subconciously, but his superiority was so predominant that his games normally concluded with a display of his superlative combinative powers. Steinitz's tactical skill was not so great and he therefore had to win by the use of superior strategy. By so doing he created the foundations of modern chess.

3) *Steinitz–G. A. MacDonnell*
Dublin 1865
Philidor Defence

| 1 P–K4 | P–K4 |
| 2 N–KB3 | P–Q3 |

An inferior defence, playable, but certainly not suitable for beginners as Black has a cramped game. Much better is direct development of the pieces by 2 . . . N–QB3 or 2 . . . N–KB3 (Petroff's Defence).

3 B–B4

Morphy's approach was much more direct: 3 P–Q4 P×P 4 Q×P N–QB3 5 B–QN5 B–Q2 6 B×N B×B 7 B–N5, as he played in his match games with Harrwitz. A modern variation is 3 P–Q4 N–KB3 4 N–B3 QN–Q2 5 B–QB4 B–K2 6 0–0 0–0 7 Q–K2 P–B3 8 P–QR4 (to prevent . . . P–QN4) and White has a space advantage.

| 3 . . . | B–K2 |
| 4 P–B3 | |

But Steinitz's approach is quite different. He is aiming to establish a strong and secure centre. Once he has done this he will launch an attack on Black's king. Already Steinitz has one small advantage —his king's bishop has more scope than its black counterpart, a direct result of 2 . . . P–Q3.

4 . . .	N–KB3
5 P–Q3	0–0
6 0–0	B–N5?
7 P–KR3	B×N
8 Q×B	

No modern master would have exchanged his bishop in such a manner. Steinitz was the first to demonstrate the advantage of the two bishops.

| 8 . . . | P–B3 |
| 9 B–N3 | |

A far sighted manoeuvre by which Steinitz preserves his king's bishop, the point becoming apparent on move 11.

9 ...	QN–Q2
10 Q–K2	N–B4
11 B–B2	N–K3
12 P–KN3	

Preparing to support the advance P–KB4

12 ...	Q–B2
13 P–KB4	KR–K1
14 N–Q2	QR–Q1
15 N–B3	K–R1 (*116*)

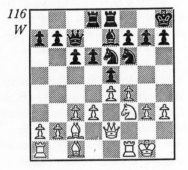

Black is in trouble and tries to organise his defence against the coming storm on the K-side. He has no counterplay in the centre to distract White from his operations against his king.

16 P–B5	N–B1
17 P–KN4	P–KR3
18 P–N5	P×P
19 N×NP	K–N1
20 K–R1	

The contrast between the two king's moves is instructive. White is preparing to place his rooks on the open king's knight file and so moves his king out of the way; Black's a defensive shuffle. It is apparent how short of space Black has become.

20 ...	NB3–R2
21 N–B3!	

Quite rightly avoiding an exchange which would help to relieve his cramped opponent.

21 ...	R–Q2
22 R–KN1	B–Q1
23 B–R6	P–B3
24 R–N2	P–Q4 (*117*)

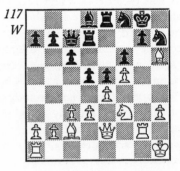

Black has organised a cumbersome defence of his KN2. Nevertheless he realises that White can reinforce his pressure decisively by such moves as QR–KN1, B–N3+, N–R4 and Q–R5. He therefore tries to free his position by advancing in the centre. But Black's pieces are so tangled up that White can take tactical advantage of their poor position.

25 QR–KN1	RK1–K2
26 P×P	P×P
27 B–R4	R–Q3

Otherwise simply B×R; but now KN2 is inadequately protected.

28 R×P+	R×R
29 R×R+	Q×R
30 B×Q	

and White won

An impressive game. White's victory stemmed from the fact that Steinitz had a logical plan, while his opponent had none. The closed nature of the position is typical of Steinitz and in direct contrast to Morphy.

Dr Siegbert Tarrasch
1862–1934

If Steinitz was the thinker who created the theoretical framework on which modern chess is played, it was the German master Tarrasch who was the teacher of the generation of masters who followed Steinitz. A leading master for over thirty years, Tarrasch scored many tournament triumphs in his long chess career, but he never won the world title. However, Tarrasch's formidable reputation in the chess world rested not only on his great playing skill, but also on his writings. Tarrasch was a very fine writer whose clarity of thought and expression make his text books amongst the finest in chess literature. Tarrasch basically followed Steinitz's thinking, but he emphasised the value of rapid and economical development and was a specialist in the art of constricting an opponent until his position collapsed.

4) *Tarrasch–Dr Noa*
   Hamburg 1885
   French Defence

1 P–K4	P–K3
2 P–Q4	P–Q4

The difficulties that Black experiences in many variations in defending his king's pawn after 1 P–K4 P–K4 led to a search for alternative methods of development. One of the most reliable of these is the French Defence. It is at once apparent that White lacks an obvious target and must adopt a strategy quite different from the open games characterised by 1 P–K4 P–K4.

3 N–QB3

White's king's pawn is attacked and he must do something about it. The obvious move is 3 P–K5 setting up a pawn chain. This move creates an outpost, which if it can be maintained, normally gives White the advantage. But Black can launch an immediate and vigorous counter-attack by 3 ... P–QB4 and 4 ... N–QB3 followed by ... KN–K2–KB4 and can secure equality. White does better to maintain the tension in the centre.

3 ...	N–KB3

The major alternative is 3 ... B–N5 creating a pin on the knight at QB3, known as the Winawer

Variation. 3 . . . P×P is playable, but demands great accuracy from Black to obtain an equal game as it cedes the superiority in the centre to White.

4 P–K5

In vogue at the time, but 4 B–KN5 maintaining the tension in the centre is a little stronger.

4 . . .   KN–Q2
5 NB3–K2

An ambitious move whose aim is to reinforce the centre by P–QB3. Nevertheless the loss of time is too great and Black can gain the advantage. Better is Steinitz's move 5 P–B4 P–QB4 6 P×P N–QB3 7 N–B3 B×P 8 B–Q3 P–B3 with chances for both sides.

5 . . .   P–QB4
6 P–QB3   N–QB3

The refutation of White's fifth move, discovered many years later, is 6 . . . P–B3 7 P–KB4 P× QP 8 BP×P P×P 9 BP×P B–N5+ and if 10 B–Q2 or 10 N–QB3 10 . . . Q–R5+ with advantage. An instructive variation showing how White's seemingly formidable centre has been undermined by Black's vigorous counter-attack.

7 P–KB4   P×P

Not good; 7 . . . Q–N3 is Tarrasch's recommendation followed by . . . P–B3 and . . . 0–0.

8 P×P   B–N5+
9 B–Q2!

Perhaps Black was relying on 9 N–QB3 with the following variation: 9 . . . 0–0 10 N–B3 P–B3 11 B–Q3 P×P 12 BP×P R×N! 13 P×R Q–R5+ 14 K–B1 N×QP 15 P–B4 Q–R6+ 16 K–B2 B–B4 17 B–K3 N×P! 18 P×N B–Q2 followed by 19 . . . R–KB1+ winning. Once again Black has caught White out before he has completed his development. But Tarrasch's move is an improvement and refutes Black's play.

9 . . .   Q–N3
10 N–KB3   0–0
11 B×B   Q×B+
12 Q–Q2

Offering the exchange of queens because, as we shall see, the endgame is very unfavourable for Black.

12 . . .   N–N3
13 N–B3   R–Q1
14 N–QN5

Dealing with the threat of 14 . . . N–B5 15 B×N P×B and the QP is attacked, but now White can play 16 N–Q6.

14 . . .   B–Q2
15 N–Q6   RR1–N1
16 R–B1   Q×Q+
17 K×Q *(118)*

With this exchange, the first part of the game is concluded and in White's favour. Black has been unable to shake White's grip on the centre and is rather cramped as a result. Furthermore, Black's queen's bishop is badly placed, blocked by his own pawns. It should be noted that White's king is well placed in the centre of the board.

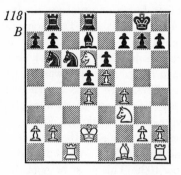

17 ...   N–B1?

Wishing to exchange the advanced knight.

18 N–QN5!

But White correctly avoids the exchange. Black should therefore have played 17 ... P–QR3 before ... N–B1 and thereby forced the exchange.

18 ...	P–QR3
19 N–B3	NB1–K2
20 B–Q3	RN1–B1
21 P–QN3	

Aiming to play 22 N–QR4, followed by N–B5, which would be wrong at once as the N would have been *en prise* on QR4.

21 ...	N–N5
22 P–QR3	NN5–B3
23 P–QN4	

Black's manoeuvre has forced White to postpone 23 N–QR4 as there would follow 23 ... N–R4 24 N–B5 R×N 25 P×R N×P+. This variation was the point behind Black's last two moves.

22 ... N×B would have been to White's advantage as the knights are better than the bishops in this type of position. Now follows a quiet period of manoeuvring as White strengthens his position and prepares for an advance on the K-side.

23 ...	P–R3
24 P–KR4	N–N1
25 K–K3	R–B2
26 R–B2	R1–QB1
27 R1–QB1	K–B1
28 P–N4	B–K1
29 N–Q2	N–Q2
30 N–N3	N–QN3
31 N–B5	N–B5+

Not good, but Black has no sensible defence against White's plan to launch an attack on the K-side.

32 B×N	P×B
33 N5–K4	P–QN4
34 N–Q6	R–N1 (*119*)

White has built up an impressive position and now launches his carefully prepared K-side attack.

35 P–B5   B–Q2

36 R–B2	N–Q4+
37 N×N	P×N
38 P–N5	

White steadily continues to gain ground.

38 ...	P–KR4
39 R1–B1	K–N1
40 P–N6	

However Black plays, White will now open a file and penetrate along it with his rooks.

40 ...	P–B3
41 R–K2	B–B3
42 R1–K1	R–Q1
43 K–B4	P×P+
44 R×P!	K–B1
45 N–B7	R–K1
46 N–N5	R2–K2?

A blunder that loses at once, but Tarrasch gives the following analysis which shows how hopeless Black's game had become: 46 ... R×R 47 P×R! R–K2 48 P–B6 P×P 49 P×P R×R 50 N–R7+ K–K1 51 P–B7+ K–Q2 52 P–B8=Q R–KB8+ 53 K–N5 R×Q 54 N×R+ K–K2 55 P–N7 K–B2 56 K–R6 K–N1 57 N–N6 and wins.

47 N–R7+	1–0

A game typical of Tarrasch's method, and particularly creditable as it was his first game in a major international tournament.

Dr Emanuel Lasker
1868–1941

When Steinitz lost the title to the young German master, Lasker in 1894, the chess world did not readily comprehend that this was the start of the longest reign of any world champion. Lasker retained his title in matches against Steinitz, Marshall, Tarrasch and Schlechter. In tournaments he was wonderfully successful. Perhaps his greatest feat was, at the age of 67, third place, undefeated, only half a point behind the winners Bovtinnik and Flohr (40 years his junior) in the mammoth international tournament, Moscow 1935. This must be regarded as one of the finest of all chess performances.

Lasker's greatness lay not only in his magnificent tactical skill and superb endgame play, but also in his uncanny ability to play the man as well as the board. A wonderful fighter (no player ever won so many lost games as Lasker) he remains to this day a unique and isolated figure. Lasker created no school and left no immediate disciples.

Perhaps the most remarkable feature about Lasker, a mathematician and philosopher of distinction, was that he often neglected chess for several years, before returning to match play as strong as ever. No other master has been able to do this.

In view of all this, is it any wonder that a later world champion, Dr Euwe, wrote in an appreciation: 'One can only stand and wonder'.

5) *Chigorin–Lasker*
St. Petersburg 1895–6
Evans Gambit

1 P–K4	**P–K4**
2 N–KB3	**N–QB3**
3 B–B4	**B–B4**
4 P–QN4	

One of the most famous gambits on the chess board, invented by an English amateur, Captain Evans and named after him. It leads to brilliant and dashing play if Black attempts to hold on to his material advantage. White gives up a pawn, in order to occupy the centre and gain time.

4 . . .	**B×NP**
5 P–B3	**B–B4**
6 0–0	**P–Q3**
7 P–Q4	**B–N3!**(*120*)

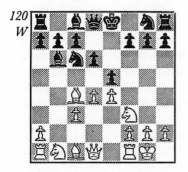

120
W

Lasker's defence, which has more or less put the Evans Gambit out of business. Black is prepared to return the pawn, 8 P×P P×P 9 Q×Q+ N×Q 10 N×P B–K3 for a satisfactory position with prospects of exploiting White's weak Q-side pawns. But Lasker's defence also has a psychological

basis. White has offered a pawn hoping for an attacking game; instead he is given the alternative of reaching a 'dull' endgame, or, sacrificing a pawn for an inadequate attack. And Lasker knows that his opponent, a romantic attacking player in the style of Anderssen, will prefer the latter.

8 P–QR4	**N–B3**

A very effective reply. It is apparent that White does not have much of a lead in development for his pawn.

9 B–QN5

If now 9 . . . 0–0? 10 B×N P×B 11 P–R5 etc.

9 . . .	**P–QR3**
10 B×N+	**P×B**
11 P–R5	**B–R2**
12 P×P	**N×P**
13 Q–K2?	

Once again playing for attack. He could regain his pawn by 13 Q–R4 N–B4 14 Q×P+ B–Q2 15 Q–Q5 0–0 and White has the worse game but he might scramble out with a draw.

13 . . .	**P–Q4**
14 N–Q4?	

Possibly an overnight or a last attempt to complicate the game.

14 . . .	**N× QBP!**
15 N×N	**B×N**
16 Q–Q3	**P–QB4!**

The ending after 16 . . . B×N 17 Q×B would be difficult to win owing to the bishops of opposite colour e.g. 17 . . . B–Q2 18 B–R3.

17 Q–N3	**B–K3!**

Black could not castle because
17 ... 0–0 18 B–R6 B×KP 19
Q×B P×B   20 N×P. Now 18
Q×P? would expose White to a
strong attack on the king's knight
file after 18 ... K–Q2 19 Q–N3
R–KN1 with play similar to the
game Black's king is quite safe in
the middle of the board protected
by his pawns and his, by now,
superior development.

18	B–N5	Q–Q2
19	QR–B1	P–KB3!
20	P×P	P×P
21	B–B4	R–KN1
22	Q–B3	0–0–0

Black's game has steadily improved during the last few moves
and he will soon move over to the
attack.

23	KR–K1	P–B5

White threatened 24 Q–K2
B–B4 25 Q×P+ and wins.

24	Q–K2	B–KB4
25	Q–R2?	*(121)*

The final mistake, but in the
long run his position is lost. Now
Lasker destroys White's position
by a sacrifice.

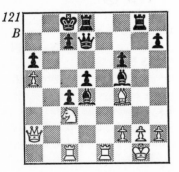

25 ...   R×P+!
26 K–R1

Or 26 K×R B–R6+ 27 K–R1
Q–N5 wins.

26 ...   R×BP
   0–1

White resigns, for if 27 N–K2
B–K5+ or if 27 B–Q2 Q–Q3.
Lasker conducted the defence
with iron strength. Games such
as this were the graveyard of the
romantic attacking style.

José Raoul Capablanca
1888–1942

Few, if any, chess players had a
greater natural genius for the
game than the Cuban, Capablanca. A boy prodigy, champion
of Cuba at 12, he burst upon the
chess world by winning his first
international tournament at San
Sebastian 1911. The inevitable
match with Lasker came in 1921.
This proved to be a disappointing
affair, as Lasker failed to show
any of the fighting spirit which
was such a characteristic of his
style, Capablanca winning decisively.

No player has ever equalled
Capablanca for the faultless accuracy of his play; in his whole
career he only lost 36 games. As
a pure position player, Capablanca remains unmatched; he
was also one of the finest endgame
players in chess history. Nor could
he be shaken by complications—

he analysed the most complex positions with unrivalled speed and accuracy.

Truly a great chess player; but his natural talents caused him to neglect the study of the openings and this was to prove his Achilles heel in his match with Alekhine. After the loss of the title, Capablanca's best days were over and he came to rely more and more on his technique, though he remained to the end of his life one of the best players in the world.

6) *Capablanca–H. Steiner*
Budapest 1928
Queen's Gambit Declined

1 P–Q4	N–KB3
2 P–QB4	P–K3
3 N–QB3	P–Q4
4 B–N5	QN–Q2
5 P–K3	B–K2
6 N–B3	0–0
7 R–B1	P–B3
8 B–Q3	P×P
9 B×BP	N–Q4

The players are following the main variation of the Orthodox Defence to the Queen's Gambit Declined. By his last move Black forces an exchange that relieves his cramped position.

10 B×B	Q×B
11 0–0	N×N
12 R×N	P–QN3?
	(122)

Black's idea is to develop his game by ... B–N2 and ... P–QB4 but Capablanca shows that,

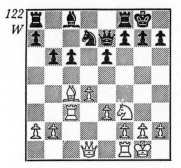

however reasonable the intention, it is in fact a mistake. The correct move is 12 ... P–K4 and if 13 P×P N×P 14 N×N Q×N 15 P–B4 Q–B3! and despite intensive analysis an advantage for White has not been demonstrated.

13 Q–B2!   **P–QB4**

White's last move threatened to win a pawn by 14 B–Q3. If 13 ... B–N2 14 B–Q3 P–N3 (or 14 ... N–B3 15 N–K5 with the same result) 15 B–K4 winning the QBP.

14 P×P!   **N×P**

14 ... P×P 15 B–N5 wins the QBP.

15 P–QN4!   **N–R3**

A wretched retreat, but the retreat to Q2 loses as follows:

16 B–Q3! and now:

a) 16 ... Q×P? 17 B×P+ K–R1 18 R–B4 Q–K2 19 R–KR4 with a winning attack.

b) 16 ... P–N3 17 R–B7! with many threats e.g. 17 ... Q×P 18 Q–B6.

16 P–QR3	B–N2
17 B–Q3!	P–N3

18 R–B1!

Now Black finds that his obvious defence 18 ... QR–B1 loses to 19 R×R R×R 20 Q×R+ B×R 21 R×B+ K–N2 22 B×N, so White has gained control of the QB-file.

18 ...	QR–Q1
19 N–K5	

Once again gaining time: Capablanca threatens B×N followed by N–B6.

19 ...	Q–Q3
20 P–B4 (*123*)	

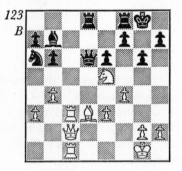

123
B

An obvious move, protecting the knight. But there is more to it than that: Capablanca has prepared a beautiful variation if Black tries to free himself by 20 ... P–B3 21 N×P! P×N 22 B×N B×B 23 Q×P+ K–R1 24 P–N5!! (Not 24 P–K4? Q–Q5+ and Black forces mate) 24 ... B×P (or 24 ... B–N2 25 P–K4 Q–Q5+ 26 K–B1 and wins) 25 Q–R5+ K–N2 26 Q×B with a won game.

20 ...	N–N1
21 R–B7	B–R1

| **22 R×RP** | N–B3 |

Capablanca now concludes in impeccable style.

23 R×B!	N×N
24 R×R	R×R
25 B–K2!	Q–Q7

Once again Black has no choice 25 ... N–Q2 26 R–Q1 Q–K2 27 Q–B7 K–B1 28 B–N5 exchanging all the pieces and winning the king and pawn ending.

| **26 Q×Q!** |

Even stronger than 26 P×N Q×KP+ 27 K–R1 R–Q7 28 Q–B8+ K–N2 29 B–B3 winning a piece.

26 ...	R×Q
27 R–B8+	K–N2
28 K–B1!	N–Q2
29 R–Q8	

Forcing the win of the exchange due to pin on the Q-file.

29 ...	K–B3
30 B–N5	R–Q4

Of course after 30 ... K–K2 31 R×N+ R×R 32 B×R K×B 33 K–K2 with an easy win in the ending.

| **31 P–QR4** | R×B |

Capitulation, there is nothing better.

32 P×R	K–K2
33 R–QB8	

Of course not 33 R×N+ K×R and the ending is drawn, because of the doubled QNP.

33 ...	P–K4
34 R–B6	P–K5
35 K–K2	P–B4

36 K–Q2	K–B2
37 K–B3	1–0

A marvellous game. After his error on move 12, Black was never allowed a moment's respite. The fusion of tactics and strategy into one elegant whole shows Capablanca's style at its best.

Aron Nimzowitsch 1886–1935

Chess in the decade before the First World War was dominated by the masters who had assimilated the teachings of Steinitz and Tarrasch. A technique based on these teachings was sufficient to defeat other players without much effort. Master chess of the pre-war era often lacked initiative and fighting spirit—many of the games between the leading masters were short draws.

However, after the war, the views of the Tarrasch school were challenged by a group of young players who rapidly proved that there were many exceptions to Tarrasch's rather dogmatic teachings. Leaders of the movement were Alekhine, Bogoljubow, Breyer, Nimzowitsch and Reti. Though the Hypermoderns, as this school came to be known, overstated many of their ideas, they brought a much needed liveliness to international chess.

The deepest thinker of the group was Aron Nimzowitsch who formulated his theories in his remarkable book, 'My System'. A world class player for many years, he never obtained the world title match he deserved.

One of the major disagreements between the two schools was the treatment of the centre. The Hypermoderns demonstrated that the centre need not be occupied by pawns, but that it could, on occasion, be held by the pieces. The following game, the first where this strategy was deliberately followed by one player, created an immense controversy at the time. The reader should contrast Nimzowitsch's and Tarrasch's treatment of the French Defence.

7) *Nimzowitsch–Salwe*
   Carlsbad 1911
   French Defence

1 P–K4	P–K3
2 P–Q4	P–Q4
3 P–K5	P–QB4
4 P–QB3	N–QB3
5 N–B3	Q–N3
6 B–Q3 (*124*)	

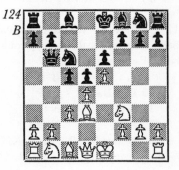

124
B

Already a critical position has been reached. White has tried to establish a pawn chain in the centre and Black has launched an immediate counter attack on white's QP. At the moment White has the pawn protected indirectly: 6 ... P×P 7 P×P N×QP? 8 N×N Q×N 9 B–QN5+ wins the queen. So Black makes a very plausible move, which sets up the threat by stopping 9 B–QN5+. But 6 ... B–Q2 is a mistake. Black should play 6 ... P×P fixing the pawn position and then play 7 ... B–Q2.

6 ...   **B–Q2**
7 P×P!

One of the most controversial moves ever played.

7 ...   **B×P**
8 0–0   **P–B3**

In accordance with the theory of the times, Black falls upon the remaining member of White's pawn chain. Better would have been 8 ... P–QR4 maintaining the bishop's good position.

9 P–QN4!

Very strong, driving the bishop back, 9 Q–K2 P×P 10 N×P N×N 11 Q×N N–B3 would not have been so good as the queen could be easily forced away.

9 ...   **B–K2**
10 B–KB4   **P×P**
11 N×P   **N×N**
12 B×N   **N–B3**

The desirable 12 ... B–KB3 fails against 13 Q–R5+ P–N3 14 B×P+ P×B 15 Q×P+ K–K2 16 B×B+ N×B 17 Q–N7+.

13. N–Q2!

Nimzowitsch points out that it would be wrong to win a pawn by 13 Q–B2? 0–0 14 B×N R×B 15 B×P+ K–R1 16 B–Q3 as White has given up the blockade on the centre and after 16 ... P–K4 Black would have good compensation for his pawn.

13 ...   **0–0**
14 N–B3   **B–Q3**
15 Q–K2!

Once again Nimzowitsch plays most accurately: If 15 B–Q4 Q–B2 16 Q–K2 N–N5 17 P–KR3 P–K4! and Black wrecks the blockade.

15 ...   **QR–B1**

Perhaps the passive 15 ... QR–K1 and 16 ... B–B1 would have been better; but Black's position has obviously become unsatisfactory.

16 B–Q4   **Q–B2**
17 N–K5   **B–K1**
18 QR–K1 (*125*)

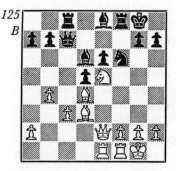

125
B

It is now apparent how badly cramped is Black's position. His centre is completely blockaded by the white pieces. Nimzowitsch now has little difficulty in building up an attack on the black king.

18 ...	B×N
19 B×B	Q–B3
20 B–Q4	B–Q2
21 Q–B2	

Threatening 22 B×N and 23 B×P+

21 ...	R–KB2
22 R–K3	P–QN3
23 R–N3	K–R1

Hoping to defend himself after 24 B×N by 24 ... P×B but:

24 B×RP!	P–K4!

If 24 ... N×B 25 Q–N6 K–N1 26 B×KNP N–B1 27 Q–R6 N–R2 28 B–B6+ and wins. Black finds the best reply which frees his game to some extent; but the damage has been done to his king's position and White's pieces are too well placed to be seriously disturbed by Black's efforts. The student should compare this position with that given in the note to White's 13th move and he will appreciate the damage done to Black's position.

25 B–N6	R–K2
26 R–K1	Q–Q3
27 B–K3	P–Q5
28 B–N5	R×P
29 R×R	P×R
30 Q×P	K–N1
31 P–QR3	K–B1

32 B–R4	B–K1
33 B–B5	Q–Q5

Transposing into a lost ending, but otherwise 34 B–N3 would have won more material.

34 Q×Q	P×Q
35 R×R	K×R
36 B–Q3	K–Q3
37 B×N	P×B
38 K–B1	B–B3
39 P–KR4!	1–0

Black has no satisfactory defence against the advance of the passed KRP. As Nimzowitsch himself wrote: 'A most instructive game from A to Z'.

Dr Alexander Alekhine
1892–1946

The man who succeeded Capablanca was a very different kind of master from the Cuban. Alekhine reinforced his gifts by incessant study and became the outstanding theoretician—especially of the openings—of his generation. He mastered all types of play, but his speciality was the build up and creation of attacking positions. Once Alekhine achieved an attacking position his superb combinative gifts came into full play—often overwhelming his opponent with a dazzling series of blows. In his best years 1929–1934 Alekhine dominated the chess world. He twice defended his title successfully against Bogoljubow, but then surprisingly lost it to the Dutchman, Dr Euwe in 1935, only to regain the title in a return match in 1937.

At the end of the 30's it was apparent that a younger generation of masters was challenging Alekhine for the title, but World War II prevented a match being arranged. When Alekhine died in 1946, the world title was left vacant for the first time since 1886.

In the following characteristic game we see Alekhine at his best. The manner in which he builds up his attack is most impressive. A comparison with Anderssen's victory over Rosanes, shows how much chess technique improved in the intervening years.

8) *Stahlberg–Alekhine*
   Hamburg 1930
   Nimzo-Indian Defence

1 P–Q4	**N–KB3**
2 P–QB4	**P–K3**
3 N–QB3	**B–N5**

By repeatedly playing this sequence of moves in master chess, Nimzowitsch showed that it was a viable defence. It is quite rightly named after him.

   4 Q–N3

As Black's defence is based upon preventing White playing P–K4 (if 4 P–K4? B×N+ 5 P×B N×P) it is logical to attack the bishop. However, the queen move is premature and Black can equalise easily.

4 . . .	**P–B4**

5 P×P	**N–B3**
6 N–B3	**N–K5**
7 B–Q2	**N×QBP**

The defect of 4 Q–N3 is that Black can gain time attacking the queen.

   8 Q–B2   **P–B4**

Now P–K4 is firmly prevented.

   9 P–QR3

Nimzowitsch showed in a famous game that this cannot be delayed: 9 P–K3 0–0 10 B–K2 P–QN3 11 0–0–0 P–QR4! 12 P–QR3 P–R5! and if now 13 P×B? N×P 14 Q–N1? N–N6 mate.

9 . . .	**B×N**
10 B×B	**0–0**
11 P–QN4	**N–K5**
12 P–K3	**P–QN3**
13 B–Q3	

If he tries to retain the two bishops by 13 B–N2 there could follow 13 . . . B–N2 14 B–Q3 Q–K2! 15 B×N P×B 16 Q×P N×P 17 Q×B N–Q6+ regaining the piece with the better game.

13 . . .	**N×B**
14 Q×N	**B–N2**
15 0–0	**N–K2!**

With fine judgement, Alekhine realises the knight will be needed on the K-side.

   16 B–K2   **Q–K1**

Otherwise R–Q1 would have been unpleasant.

17 KR–Q1	**R–Q1**
18 P–QR4? *(126)*	

White's advantage certainly lies on the Q-wing and he is quite

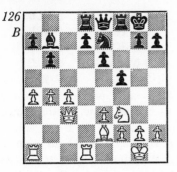

126
B

right to advance on that side of the board. But the move takes too much time and Alekhine is able to build up a decisive attack. Alekhine recommends 18 Q–K5 P–B5 19 Q–B7 B×N 20 B×B P×P 21 P×P N–B4 and White can defend himself.

18 ...   **P–B5!**

Opening the KB-file. Black's play from now on is a model of precision and accurate timing.

19 P–R5   **BP×P**
20 Q×KP   **N–B4**
21 Q–B3   **P–Q3!**

An effective defence against White's R–QR7.

22 P×P   **P×P**
23 N–K1

If 23 R–QR7 R–Q2 threatening 24 ... B×N winning a piece.

23 ...   **P–K4!**

Preparing to occupy the dominating square on Q5.

24 R–R7   **N–Q5**
25 Q–K3

He had to attend to 25 ... N×B+

25 ...   **R–Q2**

26 R–R2

A miserable retreat, but he was threatened with 26 ... B–B6!

26 ...   **R2–KB2**
27 P–B3   **R–B5**
28 B–Q3   **Q–R4**

Threats all the time: the danger is 29 ... P–K5!

29 B–B1   **Q–N4!**

And now it is 30 ... R×P! winning the queen (31 Q×Q R×B mate)

30 R–KB2 (*127*)

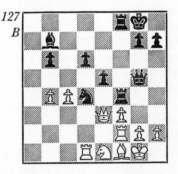

127
B

30 ...   **P–R3!**

A very fine move, based on accurate calculation. Black threatens 31 ... R×P! 32 Q×Q R×R and because the queen is attacked by the RP, White is lost as he must attend 33 ... R×B mate.

The best defence was 31 Q–Q2 B×P 32 N×B N×N+ 33 R×N R×R, 34 Q×Q R×B+ 35 R×R R×R+ 36 K×R P×Q 37 K–K2 K–B2 38 K–B3 K–K3 39 K–K4 P–N4 with a won king and pawn ending. White's next move makes no significant difference to the position.

31 K–R1   R×P
0–1

Alekhine was deservedly awarded the brilliancy prize for this fine performance. A remarkable feature of the game is that White's pawn on KB3, protected by its neighbour and 3–4 pieces, is overwhelmed and captured by the attack of the black pieces.

Dr Max Euwe Born 1901

About 1934 it became apparent that there was a slight falling off in Alekhine's play. The Dutch professor of mathematics, Euwe, was the first to take advantage of this. He defeated Alekhine in 1935 after a very exciting match 9–8 with 13 drawn, but in a return match, played two years later, Alekhine was once more in his best form and regained the title 10–4 11 drawn. Euwe remained one of the world's leading players, but after World War II, he could not match the strength of the younger Russian players. A fine writer on the game and a leading theoretician Euwe (FIDE President) now occupied a distinguished position in the chess world similar to that held by Dr Tarrasch in his later years.

9) *Euwe–Maroczy*
   Zandvoort 1936
   Queen's Gambit Declined
   1 P–Q4   P–Q4
   2 P–QB4   P–K3

3 N–QB3   N–KB3
4 B–N5   B–K2
5 P–K3   0–0
6 N–B3   QN–Q2
7 R–B1   P–B3

The same position as in the Capablanca game. In that game White played 8 B–Q3 Black replied 8 ... P×P and after 9 B×BP White has lost a tempo, so White tries to delay the development of the bishop so as to save a move.

8 P–QR3   P–KR3
9 B–B4   P–QR3

Preparing the advance of the Q-side pawns.

10 P–R3   P×P

Capturing at last, but Black now has adequate counterplay on the Q-side. This is not surprising —White has not made very effective use of his last few moves: P–KR3 and P–QR3.

11 B×BP   P–QN4
12 B–QR2   B–N2
13 0–0   P–B4
14 N–K5   P–B5?

(*128*)

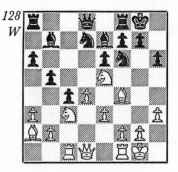

128
W

A very instructive mistake, Black releases the pressure on the centre for the sake of a Q-side majority. Black could play 14 . . . P×P 15 P×P N–N3 followed by 16 . . . N–Q4 or 14 . . . R–B1 maintaining the tension, in both cases with a good game. Now White has the advantage in the centre.

15 B–N1	**R–K1**
16 Q–K2	**N×N?**

The decisive mistake; Black cannot afford to have his knight driven from KB3. Better was 16 . . . N–B1.

17 P×N	**N–R2**
18 Q–R5	**N–B1**
19 RQB1–Q1	**Q–B2** (*129*)

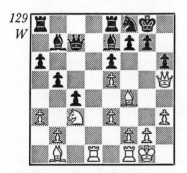

129
W

White has built up a very strong attacking position, sufficiently powerful to enable him to sacrifice a bishop to deprive the black king of his defences.

20 B×P!	**P×B**
21 R–Q4!	

The point; White threatens 22 R–N4+. Maroczy finds the only defence, which guards the second rank with his queen.

21 . . .	**P–B4!**
22 P×Pep	**B×BP**
23 R–N4+	**B–N2**
24 Q×RP	**QR–Q1**
25 N–K2!	

Another strong move, which brings the knight over to the attack

25 . . .	**P–K4**
26 N–N3	**R–K3**
27 Q–R4	**R–Q6**

Black is prepared to return the exchange to block off the dangerous bishop

28 N–B5!

Much stronger than capturing the exchange, which would give Black a strong passed pawn. It is nearly always better to pursue an attack than to make a premature gain of material.

28 . . .	**N–N3**
29 Q–R5	**Q–B2**
30 P–KR4!	

The decisive strengthening of the attack: White threatens to move his queen and advance his rook's pawn with decisive effect.

30 . . .   **B–KB1**

Or 30 . . . K–B1 31 N×B K×N 32 P–B4–B5 and wins.

31 N–R6+	**B×N**
32 Q×B	**Q–R2**
33 Q–N5	**K–B2**
34 B×R	**P×B**
35 Q–B5+	**1–0**

Black resigned because if 35 . . . K–K2 36 P–R5 N–B1 37 Q×Q+

N×Q 38 R–N7+ wins, and if 35 ... R–KB3 36 Q–Q7+ K–N1 37 Q–K8+ K–N2 38 Q–K7+ R–B2 39 Q×P+ K–B1 40 Q–Q6+ and 41 Q×QP with an overwhelming pawn mass.

An interesting game, finely played by Dr Euwe, which illustrates the defensive value of the pawns in front of the castled king. Despite having all his pieces in play, Black was unable to organise a satisfactory resistance.

Dr Mikhail Botvinnik
Born 1911

Alekhine's death in 1946 left the world title vacant. The International Chess Federation (FIDE) took the opportunity to take over control of the championship, and organised in 1948 a tournament for the title. This was very decisively won by the Russian Botvinnik, the outstanding representative of the leading chess nation.

The world champion now has to defend his title in a 24 game match every three years. His opponent earns the right in a series of representative tournaments and matches and there is nothing to prevent any player earning the privilege of a title match if he is good enough—a vast improvement on the old haphazard system of challenges by individual players when the title was the personal property of the champion. As a result Botvinnik defended his title in a series of memorable matches.

Botvinnik is a player strong in every phase of the game. A deep strategist and fine combinative player; an opening theorist and outstanding endgame virtuoso; it is difficult to find a chink in Botvinnik's armour. A distinguished electrical engineer, Botvinnik brings a scientific approach to chess. Not the least reason for Botvinnik's success is his determination and formidable self control.

10) *Botvinnik–Smyslov*
World Ch, Moscow 1954
Slav Defence

| 1 P–Q4 | P–Q4 |
| 2 P–QB4 | P–QB3 |

We have seen how in many variations of the normal Queen's Gambit Declined Black's major problem is the development of his queen's bishop (vide Capablanca's game). The Slav Defence is an attempt to avoid these difficulties as Black has not blocked in his bishop by 2 ... P–K3. Nevertheless the move has its defects: it is not a developing move, nor does it add pressure to the centre. The Slav Defence has never had sustained popularity and its main exponent in master chess is Smyslov.

| 3 N–KB3 | N–B3 |
| 4 N–B3 | P×P |

5 P–QR4

Forced, unless White wants to play a gambit by 5 P–K4 P–QN4 when Black retains his pawn. Now Black can develop his queen's bishop.

5 ...	B–B4
6 P–K3	P–K3
7 B×P	B–QN5
8 0–0	QN–Q2
9 N–R4	

So far the main variation of this defence 9 Q–K2 is normally played, but Botvinnik's move has the aim of occupying the centre by P–B3, P–K4 and exchanging the knight for bishop, thus obtaining the advantage of the two bishops.

| 9 ... | 0–0 |
| 10 P–B3 | |

Much better than 10 N×B P×N when Black's firm hold on K5 gives him a good game.

10 ...	B–N3
11 P–K4	P–K4
12 N×B	RP×N
13 B–K3	Q–K2
14 Q–K2	P×P
15 B×QP	B–B4
16 B×B	Q×B+

17 K–R1 (*130*)

During the last few moves Black has freed his game by a series of exchanges and appears to have equalised. Nevertheless White has still retained some advantage. Firstly his bishop is obviously an excellent piece; secondly he has control of the centre

and threatens to advance his pawns driving back the black knights. It is certainly impressive how Botvinnik blends these hardly perceptible advantages into victory.

17 ...   **P–KN4**

A weakening move that was perhaps best avoided. Black's aim is to provide squares for his knights at K4 and KB5 but as he fails to achieve this aim the move should have been replaced by 17 ... QR–Q1. White would continue in similar fashion to the game.

18 P–KN3	QR–Q1
19 B–R2	KR–K1
20 QR–Q1	N–B1
21 R×R	

Diverting Black's remaining rook from the K-side. Black can make no use of the open file as he has no points of entry on it.

| 21 ... | R×R |
| 22 P–K5 | N–Q4 |

Moving the knight elsewhere is equally unattractive.

| 23 N×N | P×N |

24 Q–Q2	N–K3
25 P–B4	

A very powerful move. The further advance of the KBP will disrupt Black's defences. Despite having only three pieces available Whit's K-side attack has tremendous force—a tribute to Botvinnik's careful preparation.

25 ...	P×P
26 P×P	Q–B3
27 P–B5	N–B4
28 Q–N5	R–Q2?
	(131)

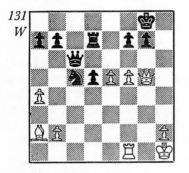

131
W

This allows White to win a piece; a better defence was 28 ... P–B3 but after 29 Q–N2 Black remains with a very poor game.

29 R–KN1	P–B3
30 P×P	N–K5
31 P–B7+	

The refutation of Black's last move.

31 ...	R×P
32 Q–Q8+	K–R2
33 B×P	N–B7+
34 K–N2	Q–B3
35 Q×Q	R×Q

36 K×N	R×P+
37 B–B3	R–B5
38 R–N4	1–0

A beautiful game by Botvinnik. The value of the game is enhanced by the play of the loser: it is extremely difficult to tell where Smyslov made the decisive mistakes. This game was played in a world championship match —it says much for Botvinnik's character that he could play such beautiful chess after scoring only one draw from the previous five games.

Vasily Smyslov Born 1921

Botvinnik defended his title for the first time in 1951, drawing 12–12 against his Russian colleague Bronstein. His second match in 1954 was against another Russian master, Smyslov. This too was drawn. Three years later Smyslov once again earned the right to a world title match. This time Smyslov was successful, winning 12½–9½. But he lost the title in a return match a year later 10½–12½.

During his best period in the mid 1950's, Smyslov's play showed a massive solidarity. A near impregnable defence supported by remorseless end game play brought him a remarkable series of successes.

In order to appreciate the next game, it is important to know a little of the circumstances under which it was played. Smyslov's opponent, one of the strongest players never to win the world title, needed to win this game in order to overtake Smyslov in the tournament placings—and the tournament winner would play Botvinnik for the title.

11) *Keres–Smyslov*
   Zürich 1953
   Queen's Indian Defence

1 P–QB4	N–KB3
2 N–QB3	P–K3
3 N–B3	P–B4
4 P–K3	B–K2
5 P–QN3	0–0
6 B–N2	P–QN3
7 P–Q4	P×P
8 P×P	P–Q4
9 B–Q3	N–B3
10 0–0	B–N2

After various transpositions the game has reached a well known position in the Queen's Indian Defence. The normal plan for White is the manoeuvre Q–K2 KR–Q1 QR–QB1 in order to retreat the bishop to QN1. Keres has prepared a different attacking plan: QR–QB1 and KR–K1 and retreat his bishop to KB1.

11 R–B1	R–B1
12 R–K1	N–QN5
13 B–B1	N–K5

Now that the bishop has abandoned the b1–h7 diagonal, Black is able to occupy the K5 square.

| 14 P–QR3 | N×N |

15 R×N	N–B3
16 N–K5	N×N
17 R×N	(*132*)

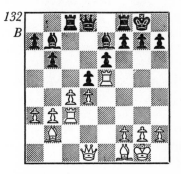

132
B

With both rooks ready to swing over to the K-side, Keres is ready to launch a fierce attack on the black king. But by his last move, Keres has crossed the rubicon and Smyslov is able to launch a formidable counter-attack on the white centre. The equilibrium of the position could have been maintained by 17 P×N P×P 18 B×P Q×Q 19 R×Q KR–Q1 etc. But Keres must play for the win and so stakes all on his attack.

17 ...	B–KB3
18 R–R5	P–N3

White already threatened 19 R×P K×R 20 Q–R5+ K–N1 21 R–R3.

19 R3–R3 (*133*)

Keres thought for half an hour before sacrificing the rook ...

| 19 ... | P×P! |

And Smyslov an equal time over the reply. If Black had captured the rook then 19 ... P×R

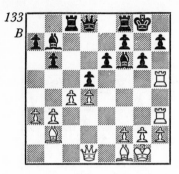

20 Q×P R–K1 and Keres would either have continued the attack by 21 P–QR4 with obscure complications, or taken the draw by repetition with 21 Q–R6 P×P 22 P–Q5! B×B 23 R–N3+ K–R1 24 R–R3 K–N1 25 R–N3+ etc. But Smyslov's move is better as it brings his QB into the defence and undermines White's centre.

20 R×P

He has no time for 20 P×P as 20 . . . P×R 21 Q×P B–K5 simply wins a rook. Or if 21 B–Q3 R–B4! 22 P×R B×B 23 B×P+ K–N2! 24 Q×P B–B8! 25 R–KN3+ K–B3 26 Q–R4+ K–K4 and the king escapes.

20 . . .   P–B6!

The winning move. If now 21 B×P R×B 22 R×R K×R.

21 Q–B1

Setting a desperately ingenious trap. If 21 . . . P×B? 22 Q–R6 Q×P 23 R–N7+ B×R 24 Q–R7 mate. But Smyslov has a simple and effective reply.

21 . . .   Q×P

White's attack has now clearly failed. Black dominates the board with his centralised pieces.

22 Q–R6

The final threat—White hopes to mate by 23 R–R8+ B×R 24 Q–R7 mate. Black avoids the threat by giving his king an escape square on KB1.

22 . . .	KR–Q1
23 B–B1	B–N2
24 Q–N5	Q–B3
25 Q–N4	P–B7
26 B–K2	R–Q5
27 P–B4	

This loses, but the position was by now manifestly hopeless.

27 . . .	R–Q8+!
28 B×R	Q–Q5+
0–1	

A master game in the best sense of the word and a classic illustration of how a premature wing attack can be defeated by a counter-attack in the centre.

Mikhail Tal Born 1936

The Latvian master Tal first burst upon the chess world when he won the 1957 Russian championship. From then on he went from one dazzling success to another, sweeping all opposition aside, culminating in a crushing victory over Botvinnik in 1960 $12\frac{1}{2}$–$8\frac{1}{2}$ for the world title itself.

Tal is an attacking player beyond fear or reproach, always prepared to sacrifice, always prepared to plunge into the most complex and obscure positions, relying on his phenominal speed of calculation to see him through. It is difficult to think of any master in chess history who can equal Tal as a tactician or attacking player.

A year later, to the surprise of the chess world, Tal lost his title to Botvinnik, once more playing in his best form. Suffering from bad health Tal has since not quite recovered the elan which brought him the world title, but he remains one of the outstanding contenders for the world title.

The following game should be considered together with that illustrating Petrosian's style. A very popular opening system is played in both games. In the first Black is triumphantly successful but in the second White holds the advantage throughout. The student should contrast the similarities and differences between the two games.

12) *Gurgenidze–Tal*
Moscow 1957
Modern Benoni Defence

1 P–Q4	N–KB3
2 P–QB4	P–B4
3 P–Q5	

The obvious reply to Black's second move, by which White gains a definite advantage in space in the centre. Black's prospects lie on the black squares and in undermining White's centre by

pawn advances on the Q-side.

3 . . .   P–K3

Considered more or less essential; the immediate fianchetto by 3 . . . P–KN3 is regarded as too passive as it allows White to play N–QB3 P–K4 P–KB4 unopposed.

4 N–QB3	P×P
5 P×P	

The alternative 5 N×P N×N 6 Q×N N–B3 7 N–B3 P–Q3 8 P–K4 B–K3 is satisfactory for Black as his pieces have good squares in the centre and the backward QP cannot be easily attacked.

5 . . .	P–Q3
6 N–B3	

An alternative system here is 6 P–K4 followed by P–B4 which leads to a very sharp game.

6 . . .	P–KN3
7 P–K4	B–N2
8 B–K2	0–0
9 0–0	R–K1

The file opened by 4 . . . P×P enables Black to put pressure on White's centre.

10 N–Q2

10 Q–B2 is an alternative that has been much analysed, but the text is probably stronger.

10 . . .   N–R3

A key move in Black's system; he plans . . . N–B2 followed by . . . P–QN4.

11 R–K1

Not a mistake, but a better move is 11 P–B3 as Petrosian played in the next game.

11 ...   **N–B2**
12 P–QR4

Delaying ... P–QN4. Experience has shown that Black at least equalises if he can gain active play on the Q side by ... P–QN4.

12 ...   **P–N3**

He cannot play 12 ... P–QR3 because 13 P–R5 blocks the Q-side.

13 Q–B2   **N–N5**

Threatening 14 ... Q–R5 White should play 14 B×N B×B 15 N–B4 with a hard game ahead. But instead he tries to drive away the knight with ...

14 P–KR3? (*134*)

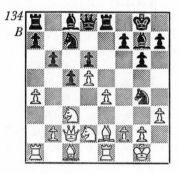

14 ...   **N×BP!!**

An astonishing sacrifice, which must have come as a complete shock to Gurgenidze.

15 K×N   **Q–R5+**
16 K–B1

If 16 P–KN3 then 16 ... B–Q5+ forces mate.

16 ...   **B–Q5**
17 N–Q1

Suddenly it becomes apparent

that all White's pieces are jumbled together. This move is the only defence against mate on KB2. But now comes a new surprise ...

17 ...   **Q×RP!**

The exquisite point being that if 18 P×Q B×RP mate! Now White's position is shattered as he cannot get his king to safety. Nonetheless it is remarkable that he lasts only another ten moves.

18 B–B3   **Q–R7**
19 N–K3   **P–B4!**

Opening lines for the attack

20 N2–B4   **P×P**
21 B×P   **B–R3!**

Creating a terrible pin on the knight at QB4.

22 B–B3   **R–K4**
23 R–R3   **R1–K1**
24 B–Q2   **N×P!** (*135*)

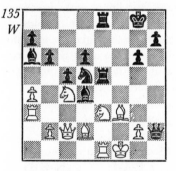

An instructive moment. All the pieces are in play. White is even a knight up; he has organised his defences as best he can; but the unsafe position of his king makes his game untenable and he succumbs to the overwhelming pressure of the black pieces. The whole position is an excellent illustration of the power of the pin.

25 B×N+   R×B
26 K–K2

Trying to escape. Other moves are equally hopeless, e.g. 26 R–K2 Q–R8+ 27 K–B2 BR3×N 28 Q×B R–KB1+ 29 K–N3 B–K4+ and 30 . . . Q–R4 mate.

26 . . .   BQ5×N
27 R×B   B×N+
0–1

After 28 Q×B Q×P+ and 29 . . . Q×B mate. The whole game is typical of Tal's genius.

Tigran Petrosian Born 1929

The Armenian Petrosian won the title when he defeated Botvinnik after a very hard match 12½–9½ in 1963. Under a revision of the world championship rules the defeated champion no longer has the automatic right to a return match and Botvinnik has now retired from active play. Petrosian successfully defended his title 12½–11½ against the Russian Spassky in 1966, but was unsuccessful when Spassky won the right to a second match in 1969, losing 12½–10½. Petrosian was crushingly defeated by Fischer 6½–2½ in the final candidates match 1971.

Petrosian's chess style is completely different from most of his predecessors. Cautious, pragmatic, careful, Petrosian is the exact opposite to Tal. His strong sense of balance in a position makes Petrosian a very difficult player to defeat.

For the first ten moves of our next game, Petrosian adopts the same moves as Gurgenidze in Game no. 12, but then he improves White's strategy. Notice how Petrosian concentrates on restricting all his opponent's counterchances before going over to the attack himself. This is typical of both the man himself and one of the best ways of playing this kind of position.

13) *Petrosian–Schmid*
   Zürich 1961
   Modern Benoni Defence

1 P–Q4   P–QB4

Schmid has made a deep study of this defence.

2 P–Q5   P–Q3
3 P–QB4   P–KN3
4 N–QB3   B–N2
5 P–K4   N–KB3
6 B–K2

Typically Petrosian does not play the more aggressive 6 P–B4 followed by 7 N–B3 known as the Four Pawns Attack.

6 . . .   0–0
7 N–B3   P–K3
8 0–0   P×P
9 BP×P

9 KP×P is not very ambitious and Black can equalise by pressure on the K-file.

9 ...	**R–K1**
10 N–Q2	**N–R3**

11 B×N is not dangerous for Black as the two bishops and open QN–file offer Black adequate counterchances.

11 P–B3!

By a different route the players have reached the same position as the previous game, but Petrosian's move is an improvement. For one thing it firmly defends his KP; it also prohibits Black's K-side counterplay and releases his pieces from the defence of the KP in order to restrict Black's Q-side. The long term plan of an advance in the centre can wait until Black's counterplay has been eliminated.

| **11 ...** | **N–B2?** |

More accurate is 11 ... N–Q2 to answer 12 N–B4 with 12 ... N–K4.

| **12 P–QR4** | **P–N3** |

If now 12 ... N–Q2 13 N–N5 is strong.

| **13 N–B4** | **B–QR3** |
| **14 B–N5** | **B×N** |

Black decides that he cannot allow the knight to remain indefinitely on QB4.

| **15 B×B** | **P–QR3** |
| **16 K–R1** | |

Tucking the king away in the corner

| **16 ...** | **R–N1** |
| **17 Q–K2!** | |

A fine move; now Black's ... P–QN4 is permanently prohibi-

ted. It is almost always a bad idea to have the queen opposite a rook on a semi-open file, but Petrosian has judged that in this instance the queen can come to no harm.

17 ...	**Q–B1**
18 B–B4	**B–B1**
19 QR–N1	**N–R4**
20 B–Q2 (*136*)	

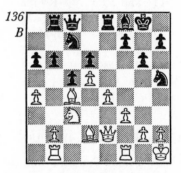

136
B

An instructive position. So far Petrosian has done little other than restrict his opponent's prospects and retain all his flexibility. As a reward he could play on either side of the board, e.g. P–QN4 taking the initiative on the Q-wing. Meanwhile, Black's position remains disjointed and it is not surprising that Schmid makes an attempt at freedom. But it is ill advised as Black's position is in no shape to cope with the open lines that result after Petrosian's surprising and vigorous reply. Better was 20 ... N–B3.

| **20 ...** | **P–B4?** |
| **21 P–KN4!** | |

Whatever Black plays open

lines result e.g. 21 ... P×NP 22
P×P N–N2   23 R–B2 and Black
is helpless against the attack along
the open KB-file.

21 ...	N–B3
22 NP×P	P×P
23 R–N1+	K–R1
24 R–N3	R–K2
25 R1–N1	R–KN2

Trying to block the open file
with 25 ... B–N2   26 P–K5!
R×P 27 Q–N2 wins for White.

26 P–K5

The decisive positional thrust,
all the more powerful for the
restraint with which White has
prepared it.

26 ...	P×P
27 Q×P	N2–K1
28 R×R	B×R (*137*)

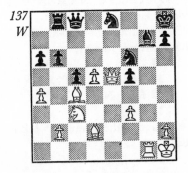

Petrosian concludes the game
with a sacrificial mating attack;
another facet of his considerable
abilities. Petrosian normally only
sacrifices when he can foresee the
outcome—in contrast to Tal.

29 R×B!	K×R
30 Q–K7+	K–N3

Or 30 ... K–R1   31 P–Q6
N–N1 32 B×N K×B 33 B–R6
and mate follows.

31 P–Q6!   1–0

An elegant final move. White
threatens 32 Q–KB7 mate and if
31 ... Q–N2   32 Q–K3! and
Black cannot avoid mate. One of
Petrosian's best games and a
model example of how to utilise
an advantage in space.

Boris Spassky Born 1937

Spassky showed his great talent
for the game at an early age,
making a successful debut at 16
and winning the grandmaster
title when only 18 years old. For
some years Spassky was over-
shadowed by Tal and Petrosian
and it was not until the 1960's
that Spassky achieved a series of
successes that established him as
the world's strongest player. Surprisingly Spassky needed two
matches to overcome Petrosian's
determined opposition, but his
reign on the chess throne proved
to be short-lived as he lost to
Fischer 12½–8½ in the sensational
match held at Reykjavik. Spassky
lost the match in the first half
winning only 1½ points out of 8
games at one stage, but he played
much better in the second and
nearly held his own. A return
match between these two great
players would be of exceptional
interest. Spassky's good manners

and dignity during the match earned him universal respect.

Spassky is the most versatile of chess players, apparently playing all types of position with equal preference. Botvinnik assessed Spassky's style as 'exceptionally universal and rational. He finds everything legible and clear ... Spassky only employs combinations and tactical ideas when it is necessary, when the position demands them.'

14) *Spassky–Ghitescu*
Beverwijk 1967
Old Benoni Defence

1 P–Q4	**N–KB3**
2 P–QB4	**P–QB4**
3 P–Q5	**P–K4**

An alternative to the 3 ... P–K3 played in the Tal and Petrosian games (pp. 117 and 119). It gives Black a difficult position as White maintains an advantage in space. Black's hopes rest upon a counter-attack by ... P–QN4 and ... P–KB4.

4 N–QB3	**P–Q3**
5 P–K4	**B–K2**
6 N–B3	**0–0**

Black's chances can best be illustrated by the game Pachman–Ciocaltea where White spoils his prospects by failing to decide on which side of the board he should concentrate his pieces: 6 P–KR3 0–0 7 B–Q3 N–K1 8 N–B3 P–QR3 9 P–QR3 N–Q2 10 P–KN4 P–KN3 11 B–R6 N–N2

12 Q–Q2 N–B3 13 N–K2? K–R1 14 N–N3 N–N1 15 B–K3 P–QN4! 16 R–QB1 P×P 17 R×P P–QR4 18 R–B2 P–R5 19 K–B1 P–B4! and Black has the initiative on both sides of the board.

7 B–Q3	**QN–Q2**
8 Q–K2	**N–K1**
9 P–KN4!	

A very strong move which prepares a powerful K-side attack. Note how firmly Spassky has prevented Black's two freeing moves ... P–KB4 and ... P–QN4.

9 ...	**P–KN3**
10 B–R6	**N–N2**
11 0–0–0	

Positions where players castle on opposite sides are characterised by fierce attacks on the opposing kings. Here White's attack is already well advanced, while Black has not even started.

11 ...	**N–B3**
12 P–KR3	**P–R3**
13 RQ1–N1	**B–Q2**
14 N–Q2	

Preparing the advance P–KR4–KR5.

14 ...	**K–R1**

Black follows the same manoeuvres as the Pachman-Ciocaltea game above, but White's attack has made so much progress that Black's position can already be considered strategically lost.

15 P–KR4	**N–N1**
16 B–K3	**P–KR4**

A weakening move, but Black

does not wish to allow P–KR5. The natural 16 . . . P–B4 was however very unattractive, e.g. 17 NP×P P×P 18 P×P N×P 19 P–KR5 followed by P–R6 and R–N7 with advantage to White. White's control over the key square K4 and the open KN-file ensures him better prospects.

17 P–N5   B–K1
18 P–B4

Forcing further concessions as Black cannot allow P–B5.

18 . . .   P–B4
19 NP×Pep

19 BP×P QP×P 20 N–B3 was also good, but Spassky has a very interesting continuation in mind.

19 . . .   N×P
20 P×P   P×P
21 N–B3   N–N5 (*138*)

Spassky now forces the play with an exchange sacrifice.

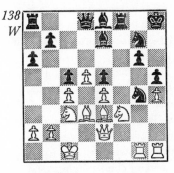

138
W

22 R×N   P×R
23 N×P   N–R4
24 N×P/N4!

A splendid move, sacrificing the other rook for the sake of dominating pawns on K5 and Q5.

24 . . .   N–N6
25 Q–N2   N×R
26 P–K5   R–B2

The alternative was 26 . . . B–Q2 27 P–K6 B×KP 28 N–K5 B–B4 29 N×P+ K–R2 30 N×R+ Q×N 31 N–K4 and White wins comfortably.

The position is very delicately balanced as the two centre pawns provide adequate compensation for the two exchanges.

27 Q×N   R–KR2

The rook defends the king, but Black is helpless in the long run against the further advance of the centre pawns.

28 P–K6   B–KN4
29 Q–K4   B×B+
30 Q×B   Q–K2
31 N–K4 (*139*)

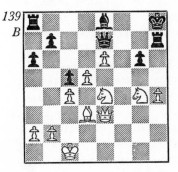

139
B

The white pieces centralise behind the centre pawns. Black is unable to bring his queen's rook into effective play. If his rook were in play—say at KB1—he would have chances of saving himself, but as it is White is able to bring superior forces to bear on the black king.

31 ...	R×P
32 NK4–B6	Q–QB2
33 B–K4	Q–R4
34 Q–KN3	P–KN4
35 N×B	RR1×N
36 Q–K5+	1–0

A rook is lost after 36 ... K–N1 37 Q×P+ K–B1 38 Q×R and the queen covers K1. A remarkable attack. Black had many alternatives after move 26, but analysis fails to reveal any satisfactory defence.

Robert Fischer Born 1943

The last five world champions have been Russians—a fair reflection of their dominance of world chess since the last world war. The Russian grip on the title was finally broken by the American, Fischer.

Very few chess players have had a greater gift for the game than the young American. Fischer ranks with Morphy and Capablanca in his ease of play and technical assurance. Unlike the great Cuban, Fischer is a chess fanatic and works at the game to the exclusion of all other interests.

It had been apparent for many years that Fischer had all the attributes of a world champion but a self destructive streak in his character, which led to endless disputes with tournament organisers prevented him from reaching the goal of a world title match. Even then Fischer nearly lost the Reykjavik match by default and was lucky to find an opponent as courteous as Spassky. Nonetheless he won the match decisively with play of the highest possible standard. Always a model opponent at the board—Fischer scorns many of the practices, such as early draws, common on the international circuit—it is a pity that his behaviour away from the board does not match his play over it.

Fischer's style is a model for any student. Basically Fischer is a position player in the classical style, but one who has an instinctive feeling for the nuances of any position. Allied to this are a rapid sight of the board, great powers of calculation, stamina and an unquenchable will-to-win. It is hard—if not impossible—to find any faults.

The game we have chosen is not from the World Championship match, as these will probably have been seen by the reader, but one played some years earlier which shows Fischer's complete mastery of chess playing.

15) *Fischer–Olafsson*
Bled 1961
Sicilian Defence

| 1 P–K4 | P–QB4 |

The most common reply to 1

P–K4. The popularity of the Sicilian rests upon the fighting game that nearly always results.

2 N–KB3	P–KN3
3 P–Q4	P×P
4 N×P	B–N2
5 N–QB3	N–QB3
6 B–K3	N–B3
7 B–QB4	

Fischer's favourite move. The bishop is undoubtedly more aggressively placed on QB4 than on K2 or KN2, but is liable to attack by the black pieces and pawns, so the move is double edged.

7 ...	Q–R4
8 0–0	P–Q3
9 N–N3	Q–B2
10 B–K2	0–0

By transposition the players have arrived in a well known variation of the Sicilian known as the Dragon. Normally Black has his pawn at QR3 and the queen at Q1. The alteration is not to his advantage. Note that White retreated his exposed bishop to K2 to avoid disclosures by such moves as ... N–K4 which bears out the comment to move 7.

11 P–B4	P–QR4

Attempting counterplay on the Q-side, but leaving a weakness on b5. Fischer's reply blocks Black's hopes.

12 P–QR4	N–QN5
13 R–B2! (*140*)	

Masterly play. Black had intended 13 ... B–K3 14 N–Q4 B–B5 15 N4–N5 Q–B1 but 16 B–

B3 and White avoids the exchange of his bishop which would otherwise be pinned against KB1.

13 ...	P–K4?

A violent attempt to free his game, which fails owing to the weakness on Q3.

14 B–B3	B–Q2
15 R–Q2	

Revealing another facet of his 13th move.

15 ...	KR–Q1
16 K–R1	

Not 16 R×P? B×P. The text move vacates KN1 for the queen.

16 ...	B–B3
17 Q–KN1	N–Q2
18 P–B5	

This advance has been calculated to a nicety. If 18 ... P×P 19 P×P B×B 20 P×B K–R1 (otherwise R–N2) 21 R1–Q1 with a clear advantage.

18 ...	P–N3
19 R1–Q1	N–B4
20 N–N5!	Q–K2

Forced; Black notices that the otherwise desirable 20 ... B×N loses the knight on N5 after 21 P×B followed by P–B3. A very neat point. Now the QP falls.

21 N×QP	N×BP
22 N×N	N×B
23 Q×N	P×N
24 B–K2	

Much better than capturing the QBP. The bishop is to be posted very strongly on QB4. The QRP is irrelevant.

24 ...	B×RP
25 P–QN3	B–K1
26 B–B4	P–R5
27 B–Q5	R×N

Olafsson gives up the exchange, believing that the resulting position will offer him good chances. The alternatives were unattractive: 27 ... R–R2 28 N×B R×N (28 ... Q×N 29 B×P+) 29 B–B6 or 27 ... QR–N1 28 N×B Q×N 29 NP×P Q×P? 30 B×P+. In both cases White retains his grip on the game.

28 B×R	R–Q5

The occupation of this strong point is the basis of Black's defence.

29 BP×P	KRP×P
30 P×P	B×P
31 R–R1	Q–B1 *(141)*

With the threat of B–R3 winning the rook and also attacking the bishop on QR8, but

32 B–Q5!!	B–R3
33 R×R	B×Q
34 R4×B	Q–R3
35 R–KB1	B–B5
36 P–N3	Q–R6

36 ... B×P 37 R–R8+ K–N2 38 R×P mate.

37 R4–R1	B×P

It is equally hopeless to allow White to capture the bishop. Black has no defence against the attack on KB2.

38 R–R8+	1–0

The queen is lost after 38 ... K–N2 39 R×P+ K–R3 40 R–R8+. A brilliant display both positionally (13 R–B2) and tactically (32 B–Q5), which well illustrates Fischer's great talents.

Bent Larsen Born 1935

The Danish grandmaster Larsen ranks with the best players in the world. Fischer and Larsen are the outstanding tournament players of the day. Larsen combines deep theoretical knowledge with considerable tactical skill. Add to this a fierce determination, a willingness to take risks and defensive play in the tradition of Lasker, and one has a most formidable master. His only weakness, over-optimism, has led to crushing defeats by Spassky and Fischer but few, other than these two players, could be considered his superior.

Larsen is a specialist in the close and restricted modern systems of development and the opportunity is taken to examine these in the last game in this section.

16) *Larsen-Geller*
Copenhagen 1960
Indian System
1 P–KN3

The aim of this move is very different from the conventional opening by 1 P–Q4. White does not intend to occupy the centre, but to develop in a quiet manner and await events. Apart from anything else, it makes it very difficult for Black to play for the draw, an important consideration to an ambitious player like Larsen.

1 ...	P–K4
2 B–N2	P–Q4
3 N–KB3	N–QB3

A further advance by 3 ... P–K5 achieves little: 4 N–Q4 P–QB4 5 N–N3 N–QB3 6 P–Q3 and White undermines Black's advanced centre. Black does better to refrain from over-extending his commitments in the centre in this kind of position.

4 0–0	N–B3
5 P–B4	

The first attack on the centre—Black must not be allowed to con-

solidate, otherwise he would obtain the better game.

5 ...	P–Q5

An aggressive move. 5 ... P×P is less committal and safer.

6 P–Q3	B–Q3
7 N–R3	

White prepares P–QN4. The advance of the Q-side pawns will help to undermine Black's centre.

7 ...	0–0
8 R–N1	R–K1
9 N–B2	P–QR4
10 P–N3	

Not 10 P–QR3 P–R5 and the Q-side advance is blocked.

10 ...	P–R3
11 P–QR3	B–KB4

11 ... Q–K2 is better, e.g. 12 P–QN4 P×P 13 P×P N×P 14 N×N B×N 15 N×KP Q×N 16 R×B Q×KP and if 17 B×NP R–N1 winning a piece. So White would proceed by 12 R–K1 to protect his KP.

12 P–QN4	P×P
13 P×P	Q–Q2
14 P–N5	N–Q1
15 P–K3!	

Attacking Black's centre once again, one defender of which (the knight at c6) has already been driven away.

15 ...	P×P
16 N2×P	B–R2
17 B–N2	P–B3
18 R–R1	R×R
19 Q×R (*142*)	

Larsen builds up the pressure on the KP. The configuration of

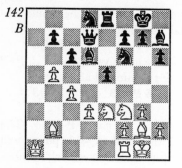

queen and bishop is quite common in openings of this type. Black cannot very well accept the offered pawn: 19 ... B×P 20 R–Q1 P–K5 21 N–K1 regaining the pawn, or 20 ... B–K7 21 R–Q2 B×N 22 B×B and White has ample compensation for the pawn. So Geller decides to surrender the KP—his last bulwark in the centre.

19 ...	**P×P**
20 N×P	**Q–B2**
21 N–B3	**B–k2**
22 R–B1	**P×P**
23 P×P	**Q–N3**
24 N–Q5	**N×N**
25 P×N	

There is now only one pawn in the centre—a white one. White clearly has the superior game as his pieces are much better placed —compare the opposing bishops. Larsen now builds up an attack on the black king during the next few moves.

25 ...	**B–B1**
26 B–Q4	**Q–N6**
27 N–K5	**P–QN4**

28 N–Q7	**B–R6** (*143*)

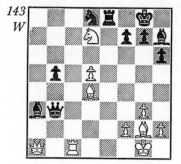

Larsen sacrifices a piece—temporarily—with decisive effect. A triumph for White's strategy on the long diagonal.

29 B×P!	**B×R**
30 N–B6+	**K×B**
31 N×R+	**K–B1**
32 Q–KR8+	**K–K2**
33 P–Q6+	**K–Q2**
34 N–B6+	**K–B1**

A real king hunt is in progress. Black cannot defend himself.

35 B–R3+	**K–N2**
36 Q×N	**B–Q6**
37 B–B8+	**K–R1**
38 Q–R5+	**1–0**

Black is mated after 38 ... K–N1 39 Q–N6+ K×B 40 Q–B7 mate.

The demolition of the black centre has been carried out with admirable skill. Rather than attempt to occupy the centre as Black did in this game, Black will come to little harm if he stakes a less ambitious claim for the centre and develops his pieces modestly but soundly.

7 In Conclusion

Improving Your Play

The first essential is regular practice against all classes of player. The best way to obtain this is to join a chess club in order to meet players of varying strengths and styles. The most satisfactory opponent is one who is stronger than you are, but not excessively so. For the player who takes chess seriously, tournament experience is essential. And he must study chess literature (see bibliography).

Chess Etiquette

We have already mentioned that a player should always adopt the 'touch move' principle, whatever kind of game he is playing. In tournament chess a player will be compelled to move the piece he has touched, whatever effect this may have upon his position. So it pays to develop the correct procedure so that it becomes automatic. If it is necessary to adjust a piece, without intending to move it, the phrase 'j'adoube' should be used before touching the piece.

Chess Clocks

All serious chess games are played under a time limit measured by chess clocks. The standard international limit for each player is 40 moves in $2\frac{1}{2}$ hours, though many matches at a lower level are played at a faster rate. A player who fails to complete his moves on time automatically forfeits the game whatever the position, so the correct handling of the clock is an important part of a player's technique. Experienced players can often play a large number of moves extremely quickly without a serious mistake, but players with less experience are advised to keep on reasonable terms with the clock.

8 Solutions to Exercises

The first move that solves a problem is called the 'key' and 'solution' may mean the whole sequence of moves or just the 'key'.

1 There are 11 solutions, namely 1 Kf7+, and all possible moves of the rook except 1 Ra7. If 1 Ra7 the game is drawn by stalemate.

2 As the king must be brought into action as quickly as possible, a first attempt might be 1 Ke3 Kg6 2 Ke4 Kg5 3 Rf2 Kg6 (Black plays to avoid being forced to a side line. But now White uses the rebound method) 4 Ke5 Kg7 5 Ke6 Kg8 6 Ke7 Kg7 7 Rg2+ Kh6 8 Kf6 Kh5 9 Kf5 Kh4 10 Rg8 Kh3 11 Kf4 (rebound method again) 11 ... Kh2 12 Kf3 Kh1 13 Kf2 Kh2 14 Rh8 mate.

A far better method is to move the rook up the f-file when the king reaches the g-file without the necessity of crossing the line of action of the rook. Hence: 1 Rf4 (Not 1 Rf5 because after 1 ... Kg6 the rook would have to move again) 1 ... Kg6 2 Kf3 Kg5 3 Kg3 and now:
a) 3 ... Kg6 4 Kg4 Kh6 5 Kf5 Kg7 6 Kg5 Kh7 7 Kf6 and mates in two moves, e.g. 7 ... Kg8 8 Rh4 Kf8 9 Rh8 mate.
b) 3 ... Kh5 4 Rg4 Kh6 5 Kh4 Kh7 6 Kh5 Kh8 7 Kg6 (Not 7 Kh6? stalemate!) 7 ... Kg8 8 Rf4 Kh8 9 Rf8 mate.

If 1 Rf4 Kg6 2 Kf3 Kg7 3 Kg3 Kg6 4 Kg4 Kh6 5 Kf5 Kg7 6 Kg5 Kh7 7 Kf6 and mate in two more moves, e.g. 7 ... Kh8 8 Kf7 Kh7 9 Rh4 mate.

3 1 Ra5 is best because it confines the black king to ranks 6, 7 and 8:
a) 1 ... Kf6 2 Kd7 Kg6 3 Ke7 Kg7 (it is no better to play to the h-file: if 3 ... Kh6 White mates in two moves by Kf7 and Rh5 mate, and if 3 ... Kh7 White mates in three moves, viz: 4 Kf7 Kh6 5 Rb5 Kh7 6 Rh5 mate) 4 Ra6 Kg8 5 Kf6 Kh8 6 Kg6 Kg8 7 Ra8 mate.
b) If Black tries to keep the white king back with 1 ... Ke7 there follows 2 Ra6 Ke8 3 Kd6 Kf7 4

Kd7 Kf8 5 Ke6 Kg7 6 Ke7 Kg8
7 Kf6 Kh7 8 Ra8 Kh6 9 Rh8
mate.

4 The principles behind this ending are as follows:
1: White retains the opposition
whenever Black threatens to cross
to the f-file, that is if the black
king is on the g-file.
2: White must not cover up his
rook by playing his king to the
f-file when the black king is on
the g-file.
3: White may relinquish the
opposition only if the black king
is on the h-file because the effort
of the king to keep the opposition
on the h-file will only be possible
if he places himself in such a
position that the rook can checkmate him.

Based on the above we get the
following solutions:
a) 1 Kh2 Kg8 2 Kg2 Kh8 3 Kf3
(not 3 Kg3 Kg7 and Black has the
distant opposition) 3 . . . Kg7 4
Kg3 Kh7 5 Kf4 Kg8 6 Kg4 Kh8
7 Kf5 Kh7 8 Kf6 Kg8 9 Kg6
Kh8   10 Rf8 mate. Naturally
fewer moves will suffice if Black
varies, e.g. 1 . . . Kh7 2 Kh3 Kg7
3 Kg3 and White has gained a
move.
b) If 1 Kg1 Kg7 and Black has
seized the distant opposition and
cannot be checkmated under the
conditions of the problem e.g. 2
Kh2 Kh6 3 Kg2 Kg6 4 Kh3
Kh5 and so on. Clearly the white

king can never play to the f-file
with the black king on the g-file,
e.g. 4 Kf3 Kf5 etc.
c) If 1 Kg2 Kg8 and Black again
has the distant opposition and can
retain it under the conditions.

5 As the position stands, the black
king can only move to one square,
namely e6. Then one of the rooks,
it does not matter which, can act
as the side line and the other can
administer mate. Therefore we
need to make a waiting move. The
position will be destroyed if the
white king or rook (f4) are moved.
Hence the solution is 1 R1f2 (or
1 R1f3) 1 . . . Ke6 2 Re2 mate.

6 1 Rb8+R×b8 2 R×b8 mate.
This type of mate on an edge rank
or file after exchanges is of
frequent occurrence.

7 1 Rg1 Kf8 2 Rf5+ Ke8 3 Rg8
mate. A simple solution is 1 Rb8
when the black rook is pinned and
if 1 . . . R×b8 2 R×b8 mate. So to
draw it out 1 Rb8 Kf8 2 R×d8+
Kg7 3 Rh1! Kg6 4 Rg8 mate.

8 Black must get rid of his rook
so as to draw by stalemate. Therefore 1 . . . Ra7+ 2 K×a7 is stalemate, and if 2 K any then 2 . . .
R×g7 also draws by equality of
forces.

9 For example 1 Kd5 Kd7 2
Qf7+ K any 3 Kc6 K any 4 Qb7,

Qc7, Qd7 or Qf8 mate according to the moves of Black's king. 4 Qf8 mate is only an alternative if the black king stands on c8 or d8.

10 1 Ng6+ Kh7 2 Be6 (waiting) 2 ... Kh6 3 Bg8 Kh5 4 Ne5 Kh4 5 Bd5 Kg3 6 Nd3 Kg4 7 Kg6 Kh4 8 Bf3 Kg3 9 Be2 Kh4 10 Kf5 Kg3 11 Kg5 Kh3 12 Nf2+ Kg3 13 Ne4+ Kh3 14 Bf1+ Kh2 15 Kg4 Kh1 16 Kg3 Kg1 17 Ba6 Kh1 18 Ng5 Kg1 19 Nh3+ Kh1 20 Bb7 mate.

There are many variations and it would be useful practice to work out how to proceed if other moves are chosen for the black king. For example, if in the above 4 ... Kh6 there might follow 5 Ng4+ Kh5 6 Kf5 Kh4 7 Kf4 Kh5 8 Bf7+ Kh4 9 Ne5 Kh3 10 Bh5 Kh4 11 Bd1 Kh3 12 Bg4+ Kg2 13 Nd3 Kf1 14 Kg3 Kg1 15 Be2 Kh1 16 Nf2+ Kg1 17 Nh3+ Kh1 18 Bf3 mate.

11 One move. Any king move except 1 Kf6 gives discovered check and checkmate. Note that 1 Kf6 would be stalemate.

12 1 Kc7 Ka8 2 K×b6 Kb8 3 Kc6 Kc8 4 b6 Kb8 5 b7 Ka7 6 Kc7 and the pawn queens.

13 Black does *not* draw by the obvious 1 ... Kg6 2 Kf4 Kf6 3 K×e4 Ke6 4 Kf4 Kf6 5 f3 and the *tempo* enables White to regain

the opposition, e.g. 5 ... Kg6 6 Ke5 and wins.

But Black can draw by 1 ... e3! 2 f×e3 Kg6 3 Kf4 Kf6 and Black holds the opposition so that White can only draw as demonstrated in the text.

14 1 Kc5 Ka8 2 Kb5 Kb7 3 a8=Q+ K×a8 4 Kc6 Kb8 5 b7 Ka7 6 Kc7 and wins.

15 1 Kc3 Kc6 2 Kd3 Kd7 3 Ke3 Ke6 4 Kf4 Kf7 5 Kf5 Ke7 6 e6 and wins.

16 1 Kg3 h5 2 e4 Kg1 3 e5 d×e5 drawn by stalemate.

17 1 ... Ke4 2 a5 (2 Kc3 is no better as the white king cannot head off the black king from his objective a8) 2 ... Kd5 3 a6 Kc6 4 Kd3 Kc7 5 Ba7 Kc6 6 Kc4 and wins because the black king can be forced so far away from the pawn that the white king can support the queening operation.

But if the pawn is at a3 instead of a4, Black draws: 1 ... Ke4 2 a4 Kd5 3 a5 Kc6 4 a6 Kc7 5 Ba7 Kc6 (now ... Kb5 is threatened and the bishop must move) 6 Bb8 (otherwise repetition of moves by 6 ... Kc7 threatening ... Kb8) 6 ... Kb6 7 a7 Kb7 drawn since Black cannot be prevented from oscillating his king between a8 and b7, and if

White plays Kb6 while the black king is at a8, then stalemate.

18 1 ... e3 2 Rf7+ Kg2 3 Re7 Kf2 4 Kd5 e2 5 Rf7+ Kg2 6 Re7 Kf2 7 Rf7+ Kg2 drawn by repetition of moves.

19 1 Qf4+ Kg2 2 Qe3 Kf1 3 Qf3+ Ke1 4 Kd4 Kd2 5 Qd3+ Ke1 6 Ke3 Kf1 7 Q×e2+ Kg1 8 Kf3 Kh1 9 Qg2 mate.

20 1 ... Ke6 2 h8=Q Qf7 mate.

21 1 a5 Bf8 2 Kd5 Bh6 3 a6 Be3 only draws. But White can improve with 1 a5 Bf8 2 g5+ K×g5 3 Kd5 and wins as the black king on g5 blocks the path of the bishop.

22 White cannot prevent the black pawn from queening, but he can create an ingenious stalemate as follows: 1 Rb7+ Kc8 2 Rb5 c1=Q 3 Rc5+ Q×c5 stalemate.

23 No, because the square c3 is not available, e.g. 1 Qa3+ Kc2 2 Qa2+ Kc1 and if 3 Kd3 d1=Q+.

24 White can castle Q-side, but not on the K-side as the bishop on c5 covers g1. Black cannot castle as he is in check. However if there is a pawn on c6 Black can castle K-side.

25 A position from actual play. Black drew the otherwise lost position by 1 ... Qg4+ 2 Kh6 (or 2 K×g4 stalemate) 2 ... Qg5+. Now White must capture the queen either with his king or queen, and stalemate results.

26 White wins a pawn by 1 B×c6 b×c6 2 d×e5 d×e5 3 N×e5. Note that 1 d×e5 N×e5 does not gain material.

27 Yes, because of the following analysis: 1 ... N×e4 and now:
a) 2 N×e4 B×h4 3 N×d6 which is White's best play.
b) 2 B×e7 N×d2 3 B×d8 N×b3+ 4 a×b3 R×d8 and Black has won a pawn.

28 From the famous game Morphy-Duke of Brunswick in consultation with Count Isouard de Vauvenargue, played during a performance of *The Barber of Seville* at the Paris Opera, 1858.

Morphy has sacrificed a piece to reach this position, the strength of which is based on the pins maintained by the bishops (b5 and g5) against the black king and queen. Black's defence is based on the knight at d7, protected by the rook at d8. Therefore Morphy played 1 R×d7 R×d7 (1 ... N×d7 2 B×e7 etc.) 2 Rd1 and now the rook on d7 is pinned in turn, and the attack reinforced by the other rook from h1. White now threatens 3 B×d7+ N×d7 4 B×e7 so Black defended with 2 . . . Qe6. White can win prosaically by 3 B×f6, but Morphy found the elegant method 3 B×d7+ N×d7 4 Qb8+ N×b8 5 Rd8 mate.

29 Won by Tarrasch in an off-hand game. 1 R×e5 R×e5 2 g3 and White wins as Black cannot break the pin on the rook, e.g. 2 . . . f4 3 g4 K moves 4 B×e5 and wins.

30 White's last move was played to relieve the pressure on c3 and anticipated the reply 1 . . . B×c3+ but Black can do better: 1 . . . Ne4 and now White succumbs to two pins. He cannot play 2 a×b4 as the pawn is pinned by the queen to the rook (. . . Q×a1+) and the pinned knight on c3 can now be captured, e.g. 2 Rc1 B×c3+ 3 b×c3 Na4 and Black wins the pawn on c3.

31 From Alekhine-Nimzowitsch, San Remo 1930. The black knight on c6 is pinned both by the bishop on b5 and by the rooks and queen on the c-file. White played 1 Ba4 threatening 2 b5 winning the knight. Black therefore played 1 . . . b5 but after 2 B×b5 Ke8 3 Ba4 Kd8 4 h4 resigned. He has only a few irrelevant pawn moves after which he will have to play . . . Qe8, when b4–b5 wins the knight.

32 No, because of the variation 1 c×d5 e×d5 2 N×d5 N×d5 3 B×d8 Bb4+ 4 Qd2 (forced) 4 . . . B×d2+ 5 K×d2 K×d8 and Black has won a piece for a pawn.

33 1 Q×b5+ a×b5 2 R×a8+ Kd7 3 R×h8 and White has won two rooks and a bishop for queen —a winning material advantage.

34 1 Bg6 Nf6 (if 1 . . . f×g6 2 N×g6+ forking king and queen) 2 B×f7 1–0 (Black resigns). Since he cannot play 2 . . . R×f7 3 Ng6+ he must lose more material.

35 1 . . . B×e4 2 R×e4 Nf2. Black's last move threatens a) . . . N×e4, b) . . . N×h3, c) . . . Nd3+ forking king and queen, and also d) . . . Rd1 mate. So 0–1 (White resigned).

36 1 Qd8+ K×d8 2 Bg5++ 1–0 as 2 . . . Ke8 3 Rd8 mate or 2 . . . Kc7 3 Bd8 mate. Won by Richard Reti.

37 Torre-Lasker, Moscow 1925. 1 Bf6 Q×h5—the black queen is unprotected, so Black must recapture, but this allows White time to set up a winning position based on the discovered check motif. Play continued 2 R×g7+ Kh8 3 R×f7+ Kg8 4 Rg7+ Kh8 5 R×b7+ Kg8 6 Rg7+ Kh8 7 Rg5+ Kh7 8 R×h5 Kg6 9 Rh3 K×f6 10 R×h6+ 1–0—Black is three pawns down. One of the few cases of Lasker being outplayed tactically, and an excellent example of a series of 'windmill' checks.

38 White has an advantage in space based upon the superior position of his pawns and pieces.

39 White has an advantage in time, as his pieces are clearly better developed. The position of the black queen c8, bishops d8 and d7 is particularly unfortunate.

40 White has an advantage in material; an extra pawn, which is sufficient to win the ending.

41 Black has an advantage in space, based not on his pawn formation, but the fact that all his pieces are posted in White's half of the board.

BIBLIOGRAPHY

The ability to record actual games has led to a very fine and extensive chess literature, much instruction—and pleasure—can be obtained by reading the best of it. The following selection, restricted to books in English currently in print is no more than an introduction to the subject.

The Openings

It is difficult, if not impossible, for any one book to deal with the ever changing field of opening theory as any fashionable variation is liable to be out of date before the book is published.

Modern Chess Opening Theory by A. S. Suetin (Pergamon) avoids this fault by concentrating on the principles behind modern chess openings. An excellent book by one of the best Russian theorists. Fine's *The Ideas behind the Chess Openings* (Bell) was outstanding when written and is now badly out of date, but is still worth reading.

Since no one player can attempt to master the whole field of opening theory he must, perforce, specialise. He should therefore, select the openings congenial to his temperament and inclinations. Batsford's 'Contemporary Chess Openings' are designed to cover this requirement. Each volume, written by a leading master, covers one opening in detail, explaining the principles behind the opening and giving the latest variations.

One other book should be mentioned: Keene's *Flank Openings* (British Chess Magazine) is an outstanding introduction to these difficult openings.

The Middle Game

Modern Ideas in Chess, Reti (Dover)
Masters of the Chess Board, Reti (Bell)
Published in the 1920s the two volumes remain amongst the finest chess books ever written. *My System* by Nimzowitsch (Bell) is one of the most influential chess books ever written; though by no means suitable for beginners, essential reading for the serious student. More suitable as a follow on from the present volume are two books by Dr Euwe: *Judgement and Planning in Chess* and, in two volumes with Kramer *The Middle Game* (*all three volumes by Bell*).

The End Game

A Guide to Chess Endings, Euwe and Hooper (Routledge)
Chess Endings: Essential Knowledge, Averbakh (Pergamon)
are two sound introductions to the subject.

Basic Chess Endings, Fine (Bell) is the classic on this part of the game.

Rook Endings Smyslov and Levenfish (Batsford) is a deep study of the most common type of ending by two famous Russian grandmasters.

Game Collections

There are many fine collections of master games. We have, of necessity, restricted our choice to post-war World Champions.

Botvinnik's Best Games 1947–1970, Botvinnik, translated by Cafferty, (Batsford).

Mikhail Tal's Best Games of Chess, Clarke (Bell)

Petrosian's Best Games of Chess, Clarke (Bell)

Spassky's 100 Best Games, Cafferty (Batsford)

My 60 Memorable Games, Fischer (Faber)

All these books contain magnificent chess and it is fascinating to compare the different ways the greatest masters go about their work. Fischer's book is outstanding and provides a unique insight into master chess.

General

The history of chess playing is a fascinating subject. Reti's two books mentioned above are the standard introductions, but stop, of course, in the 1920s. Two excellent volumes will bring the reader up-to-date:

The Development of Chess Style, Euwe (Bell)

The Battle of Chess Ideas, Saidy (Batsford)

Many of the practical problems facing a chess player are discussed in *Think Like a Grand Master* by the Russian grandmaster Kotov (Batsford).

Finally for those interested in chess problems the following two books are of exceptional interest: *Chess Problems: Introduction to an Art*—Lipton, Rice and Matthews; *The Two-Move Chess Problem*—Lipton, Rice and Matthews (both Faber).

Chess Magazines

A subscription to one of the regular chess magazines is essential for the keen player. The two established British magazines are: *The British Chess Magazine* and *Chess* whilst 'Chess Life and Review' holds a similar position in the USA. But there are many more published all over the world.

Many newspapers, both local and national, run a chess column which gives regular news, problems and games.

INDEX OF COMPLETE GAMES

INDEX OF GAME POSITIONS

INDEX OF OPENINGS